Linguistic Dis~~obedience~~

"There are too many words around to be able to say anything anymore. Censorship used to be the issue. Gagging. Now it's the spuming word geysers of social media, the non-stop jabber of reality show politicians (of which Trump is just the US example), who have occupied all language, so there is no more space for the self or for dissent. One way out is silence. Another is to reinvent how we use words, how we care for them, how we make them and they us. This short sharp book opens the conversation."
   —Peter Pomerantsev, *author of Nothing Is True and Everything Is Possible*

"This is a correctly political *Lingua Tertii Imperii* for our age. In times when the war is the words the humanities bring super-vision, this book of obedient linguistic disobedience will give you a road map—no, not a road map, let's not speak any more of road maps—it will give you a way, when there is no path, a tracery of steps taken through the mouthways of words. There will be an attentiveness awoken in your word-making tongue, as you read these disobediently obedient words, you will crave silence, as a political duty, a spiritual act."
   —Alison Phipps, *UNESCO Chair in Refugee Integration through Languages and the Arts, University of Glasgow, UK*

Yuliya Komska • Michelle Moyd
David Gramling

Linguistic Disobedience

Restoring Power to Civic Language

Yuliya Komska
Department of German Studies
Dartmouth College
Hanover, NH, USA

Michelle Moyd
Department of History
Indiana University
Bloomington, IN, USA

David Gramling
Department of German Studies
University of Arizona
Tucson, AZ, USA

ISBN 978-3-319-92009-2   ISBN 978-3-319-92010-8   (eBook)
https://doi.org/10.1007/978-3-319-92010-8

Library of Congress Control Number: 2018943808

Cover illustration: © Paul Linse / Getty Images
Cover design by Tjaša Krivec
Index by Patrick Ploschnitzki

Printed on acid-free paper

This Palgrave Macmillan imprint is published by the registered company Springer Nature Switzerland AG
The registered company address is: Gewerbestrasse 11, 6330 Cham, Switzerland

For all those who have lived and died for language

Contents

About the Authors

Yuliya Komska is Associate Professor of German Studies at Dartmouth College, USA. She wrote *The Icon Curtain: The Cold War's Quiet Border* (2015) and co-edited, with Irene Kacandes, *Eastern Europe Unmapped: Beyond Borders and Peripheries* (2017).

Michelle Moyd is Associate Professor of History at Indiana University Bloomington, USA. She is the author of *Violent Intermediaries: African Soldiers, Conquest, and Everyday Colonialism in German East Africa* (2014).

David Gramling is Associate Professor of German Studies and Second Language Acquisition & Teaching at the University of Arizona, USA. His book *The Invention of Monolingualism* (2016) received the American Association for Applied Linguistics book award for 2018.

1

Introduction: Obeying and Disobeying

This little book was conceived and written in a moment when sitting on our hands and waiting it out wasn't an option, when the need for academics and teachers to take action and a clear stand felt more important than ever in our adult lives, and when we were each personally interested in clarifying for ourselves what was and wasn't important in our stances toward language in public life. Our students, our colleagues, our children, our friends around the world—they were all asking fundamental, urgent questions of and around us, and we found we were in as good a position as anyone else to search hard for answers. To dodge the moment, its questions, and its responsibilities, because we were too busy or too jaded or too scared, sounded like the epitome of moral oblivion, the likes of which many generations before us came to regret, bitterly.

If you find something in this book that supports you, too, in listening for the questions of the age in your own hometown, neighborhood, and classroom, we will be delighted—and delighted to hear of it. None of us— Yuliya, Michelle, or David—deems herself a particularly wise or seasoned activist around any of the core questions we consider together in these pages. But we accept such inexpertise as a condition, if not a precondition, for beginning to take some of our own honest and exploratory steps toward

© The Author(s) 2019
Y. Komska et al., *Linguistic Disobedience*,
https://doi.org/10.1007/978-3-319-92010-8_1

restoring power to civic language in an age of suffering, violence, racism, outrage, and impunity. We are each haunted and moved by the general question: What kind of ancestor will you be? This is a question that such long-at-rest, treasured elders as Harriet Tubman, Václav Havel, James Baldwin, Berta Cáceres, Audre Lorde, and others contended with on our behalf, under their own darkening skies.

An initial question, then: What is linguistic *obedience?* Whether or not we instinctively favor the notion of obeying rules or people, it would be easy enough to say that being obedient in language is essentially the same as being decorous, well-behaved, orderly, moderate, even pious. Surely, in some historical eras, linguistic obedience has meant speaking in complete sentences; forming logical, doctrinaire, or prudent opinions; speaking in a way befitting one's promises, duties, and commitments; not speaking above one's station; being sparing with non-verbal cues such as gestures and eye-rolls; heeding authority; expressing oneself in a way that conveys deference and humility toward the addressee; or showing veneration toward the place and setting where one endeavors to make meaning. From Latin to Old French and onward, the etymology of obedience (*ob-,* "toward," and *audiere,* "listen") suggests an act of *hearing in the direction of* one thing, rather than another. An obedient speaker-listener hears in the direction of a given command, and not in the direction of noise, temptation, heresy, or chaos. The directional prefix "ob-" tells us that obedience is always an action of choosing one over several potential focal points of attention—a father rather than a sister, wealth rather than well-being, brute force rather than complex insight. Or, deciding to do otherwise.

Looking into the word *obey* itself (how it arose historically, as well as its current usage), we sense a conflict between two potential understandings. In the one sense, linguistic obedience may mean speaking with orderly decorum, deference, credulity, even submission—perhaps the most common understanding of obedience in its English-language meaning. In the other, directional sense conveyed by its etymology, though, obedience always implies "hearing toward power"—and thus hearing away from, or to the detriment of, other meanings potentially heard and hearable, which in the moment lack power to compel listening.

Although orderly decorum and the power to compel listening have long been culturally and economically interwoven, there is no natural connection between them. The first is a way of characterizing the speaker and her speech, while the second describes her stance toward authority and advantage. A person can exhibit one, the other, or both characteristics, but it is just as possible for his or her language to fulfill one vision of obedience, while utterly confounding the other.

And so, ours is an important historical moment to ask: what happens when power itself utters, promotes, and unleashes chaos and meaninglessness, rather than the conventionally expected forms of order and authority? When, for one reason or another, those in power outright reject the kinds of order and moderation presumed to be the default guise of bourgeois, colonial, and rationalist Liberal traditions? What happens when power claims, or appears to claim, linguistic *dis*obedience as its own native idiom, its own badge of honor, its own liberatory prerogative and outsider identity, its own tool for interactional hegemony? What stance is left for "the powerless" then? Václav Havel (1985) used this term to describe an entire citizenry under conditions of dictatorship. Are we, who live in a democracy, the latter-day "powerless" with regard to language, when the powerful have hijacked disobedience and remade it in their own image? How can we bring that image into sharper focus to help us better direct our opposition to it?

Much of our public discourse tends to view disobedience through the lens of charismatic, righteous dissent and its various cultural, political, and religious percolations—in light of which "obedience" is seen as the unrighteous, uncritical opposite. Obedient, we often take for granted, is she who speaks or writes in pat phrases, in a blandly unimposing or even ebullient tone, in compliant and normative language, while avoiding explosive, censored, taboo, or sticky questions. Obedient is he who knows when to speak and when to keep quiet, when to stick his neck out and when to regroup to see another day. Obedient are they who read from, or at least know, the scripts and lines generally expected of them, who don't ask too many questions about what the words imply, don't go searching for meaning between the lines, and neither praise nor criticize the shared language. The obedient often speak *against* their own interests, so as to not rock the boat. They reproduce coercive paradigms of thought, feeling, and identity, recycling the language of their oppressors and of past ages, despite knowing better. "Nothing will change in American politics," wrote one prominent commentator, David Green, in 2012, "so long as a majority of Americans remain linguistically obedient, passively accepting the vocabularies of politicians and media alike." Disobedience, again, appears to be the obvious critical antidote, an urgent issue for education and public health, even.

These impressions arise from a long history of critical animus toward, and veneration of, (dis)obedience—from Confucius to Virgil, from Nietzsche to Marx. In *The Eighteenth Brumaire of Louis Napoleon*, his 1852 post-mortem of the 1848 February Revolution, Karl Marx casts linguistic obedience as a kind of cognitive impairment:

> The nation feels like the mad Englishman in Bedlam who thinks he is living in the time of the old Pharaohs and daily bewails the hard labor he must perform in the Ethiopian gold mines, immured in this subterranean prison, a pale lamp fastened to his head, the overseer of the slaves behind him with a long whip, and at the exits a confused welter of barbarian war slaves who understand neither the forced laborers nor each other, since they speak no common language. "And all this," sighs the mad Englishman, "is expected of me, a freeborn Briton, in order to make gold for the Pharaohs." (65)

This image of obedience as false consciousness is a powerful and satisfying idea, one that sets up a convenient opposition between critical experts-with-insight and laypersons trapped in the hamster wheel of delusion. Easily, the first category of person gets credited with articulate and transformative awareness. But often, we find, such expert critics are simply more savvy around the predominant protocols, Liberal lineages, and "hidden transcripts"—to use James C. Scott's term (1990)—of disobeying. Correspondingly, the second group either has had no sustained recourse to the bank of such powerful ciphers and conventions, collectively dubbed "Aesopian language" by the Soviet dissident and American researcher of dissent Lev Loseff (1984), or rejects them quietly, being labeled as obedient in exchange.

Such a simplistic binary becomes even shakier if we acknowledge that experts often tend to "listen toward" (that is, obey) only a limited, charismatic range of disobedient practices. In language, many alternatives, like those cultivated in African-American Vernacular English and other critical vernaculars, are often not readily grasped by elites and pundits who are inattentive to Black meanings and styles (McWhorter 2016; Makoni et al. 2003).[1] The linguist Deborah Tannen (1981, p. 144) calls this prevalent and deeply consequential kind of interactional misrecognition "the opacity of style." Only by opening up to what is less familiar or less accessible can linguistic disobedience evolve into a more democratic practice.

Disobedience, one would expect in light of these nuances, escapes any standardized prescription. And yet, decade upon decade of its study suggest otherwise. At least since Henry David Thoreau, it has been a suspect and oxymoronic propensity of disobedience chroniclers—and those who write about them—to devise clandestine sets of virtues and dispositions, to organize and order forms of obeying and disobeying, as though the spoils of obedience were the ultimate piety to be recovered and restored. The only sanctioned course under such a scheme is to work ever harder at becoming expert, or, on the other end of things, to convert lay users of language to critical consciousness and contrary action by vigilantly dispensing how-to advice. This notion of exacting self-cultivation and mass conversion may have worked in historical settings that still traded on the ideal of maintaining elite intellectual hierarchies and their respective models of cultural stewardship—let's say, before and during the age of bourgeois revolutions and early Fordism. Recruiting for this traditional vision of linguistic disobedience will, however, reach an impasse in twenty-first century democracies, where disobedience in the guises of "creative disruption" and "outside-the-box" linguistic behavior have themselves become the go-to tools for wealthy, powerful men's repression of others.

Disobedience, in other words, is not what it used to be. Darling enfants terribles of reactionary supremacist elites, like Milo Yiannapoulos, fetishize conventional expressions of unruliness and translate them into self-aggrandizing, offensive, and pointlessly verbose autobiographies, while young activists like Emma González in Parkland, Florida, move the world with their humility, empathy, ability to "hear toward" others, to speak eloquently with and within silence. While activists like Ijeoma Oluo write books to help white people sort out their feelings around the question "What if I talk about race wrong?" (2018), the President of the United States (and the Commander in Chief of its armed forces) baldly taunts world-class athletes of color on Twitter. Little sense can be made of these inversions based on the charismatic traditional opposition between obedience and disobedience alone. But our age is not entirely unprecedented on this point. Already in 1967, Joan Didion—and before her Lionel Trilling, in different terms—foresaw similar dumbfounding and injurious truths.

She asked, then in reference to the Trump of the day, Howard Hughes: "Why have we made a folk hero out of a man who is the antithesis of all our official heroes? [...] Of course we don't admit that. The instinct is socially suicidal, and because we recognize that this is so we have developed workable ways of saying one thing and believing quite another" (2008, pp. 71–72).

Fifty years later, the elusive cleft between obedience and disobedience continues to widen in American civic life, always with language somewhere at the heart of the matter. A Washington political editor for the far-right news network Breitbart freely announced in 2017 that "the goal eventually is the full destruction and elimination of the entire mainstream media. We envision a day when CNN is no longer in business. We envision a day when *The New York Times* closes its doors. I think that day is possible" (Clark 2017). Every day makes clearer that traditional conceptions of linguistic (dis)obedience verge on impossible after Donald Trump was chosen President by 62,979,879 voting US citizens, thus throwing the already precarious New World Order of the 1990s into a bleary tailspin. Time has come to rethink these conceptions.

Antisociality: A Growth Industry

To plot the uneasy twinhood of linguistic disobedience and obedience as it has developed up until today, let us briefly consider one of Donald Trump's most unforgettable verbal *coups*—a word that here, too, refers to a seizure of power on multiple political levels. In a 2005 conversation about women with a white male reporter and member of an influential political family, Trump hypothesized that "when you're a star you can grab them by the pussy. You can do anything." Was this obedient or disobedient speech, given received definitions? According to the decorum model, consensus might be that he is performing disobedience in order to show that he can afford to actively flout traditional modes of propriety and, by this token, assert the prerogative to establish his own symbolic system, his own idiolect, his own parole—a heightened and screen-tested version, perhaps, of what the anthropologist Jane Hill (1995) described as "white linguistic disorder."

But details intercede. As Trump gets off his event bus with the reporter recording him—right after he notes with surprised self-admiration that he "can do anything"—he also says: "It's always good if you don't fall out of the bus. Like Ford, Gerald Ford, remember?" The conversation is no longer only about the dos but equally about the don'ts. Don't behave like Gerald Ford, Trump tells himself with a deflecting second-person pronoun. Ford, 40 years prior, had stumbled badly while descending the stairs of Air Force One on a visit to Austria. Preoccupied in this moment with looking foolish or indextrous in public, Trump displays a deep sensitivity for decorum and order—the semblance of which allows him, in turn, to "grab 'em by the pussy." This economy in obedience and disobedience is fueled by profound internal contradictions that we can only begin to untangle here.

But the idea of obedience as decorum and thrall to anachronistic tropes misses a more economically rational way in which this particular speaker is being utterly, cravenly obedient. At every turn, he is modeling linguistic neoliberalism in its most obedient form: prospecting for ceaseless interactional advantage, now best known by the four-letter word "deal." So much has Trump been habituated to fill every new linguistic space with tactics of advantage-accrual—through style, genre, triumph-telling, trouble-telling, adversity-talk, victim-talk, hypocrisy-baiting, elitism-baiting, birtherism-baiting, truncated performative monolingualism, and modular vernacularity—that he has become nothing if not a machine of compulsive communicative advantage, the conversational equivalent of a loan shark. Divested of decorum constraints, and infused with whatever historical discourses happen to be at hand, this is what twenty-first century neoliberal linguistic obedience looks and sounds like: its primary aim is to rack up a few stock points at every possible exchange of talk, even when not quite planning to do so.

Idioms of Domination

Loan sharks, after all, always need something to loan, some kind of credit to trade on. Harvard President Lawrence Summers (2012) suggested as much when he argued that "what you (really) need to know" in the globalized twenty-first century economy wasn't language(s) but idiom(s)—ways of speaking rather than systemic repertoires of existing meaning.

Weaponizing idioms in the service of the neoliberal master narrative of audited globalized competition, Trump becomes the spitting image of linguistic obedience, addicted to compulsive interactional capitalization through violence, hegemonic stance-taking, and style-prospecting.

In 2019, such communicative or interactional advantage accrues structurally in ways it could not even 25 years ago, and the paradigm shift is a matter of finance as much as of civic discourse. Being a committed troll—occasionally, or from cradle to grave—is of course no new vocation. But the ways in which trolling activity has been monetized since the 1990s dramatically emboldens the civic viability of hate idioms. Take Nicholas Pell, a white male language profiteer who, when writing online, "literally take[s] time to determine how [he] can phrase something in a way that will provoke the greatest amount of butthurt from sea to shining sea" (2015). This purposefulness might at first appear to be motivated by some psychosocial character trait particular to the author or his group-level identity, but it is not. Pell continues, divulging generously: "Editors know they can rely on me to produce a stream of punters giving them the sweet page views and click-throughs they need to pitch to potential advertisers. So basically every time you read my article, comment on it, and/or share it with your friends while telling them what a dick I am, you're helping me buy another pair of $400 jeans." In this consumer political economy of language, each participant's individual actions (trolling, dissenting, divesting, goosenecking, and commentating alike)—all actions traditionally understood in some way as disobedient—add up to a lucrative, credulous, and utterly obedient means of symbolic production: the monetized socialization of antisociality.

Pell's admission here is clear, proud, and, in its open-handed orientation toward "shop talk," uncharacteristically transparent—when compared for instance with the clandestine aura around Russian troll farms in journalist Adrian Chen's 2015 investigation. Pell clarifies that while he may indeed exhibit a personal or regional tendency toward "being a dick," it is not his general talent at this that keeps him in clover, but rather the ability to key his own linguistic practice to the going unit price for hate idiom. No longer is the "economic world reversed," as Pierre Bourdieu (1993) wrote about the "field of cultural production." Instead of being an intangible or "cultural" x-factor, "being a dick" is now a tradable commodity. Like any other commodity that races around the world, as consumers—indifferent, desirous, or repulsed—watch it do so, "being a dick," as Pell puts it, is a linguistic and symbolic regime that exacts, then enfranchises, its own obedient labor force. Trump is the necessarily anti-presidential expression of this alienated, accelerated labor of domination through idiom. This is what we are up against, what we must oppose.

Indivisible Language

Linguistic Disobedience is emphatically not a book about how to understand the words of Trump, his surrogates, supporters, or accessories. In fact, it started out as a short essay, published in *The Guardian* three days before Trump's inauguration, imploring all those who would listen to forget about Trump's *idiom* and take a cold, hard look at what remains of *language* (Moyd and Komska 2017). We worried that fixating on the man's pirouettes of linguistic obedience-as-disobedience—the signature anti-literate, tell-it-like-it-is, "oral" brand of ostentatious pretend-monolingualism that renders political incorrectness correct for millions, all while resuscitating the ghost of Theodore Roosevelt ("we have room for but one language here")—would leave us with nothing of our own. Dissecting his speech any more than linguists, translators, or journalists had done, we feared, would only yield to Trump another free platform, while contaminating our speech in the same breath.

And yet, the process of thinking and writing about language further has convinced us that deliberately exempting any one speaker in particular would be myopic and wishful. Sure, we can, and probably should, keep talking about the language of the right and of the left, colonizer and colonized, victims and perpetrators, men and women, white and Black, queer and straight, rich and poor. Those dichotomies harbor some useful gradations of power. The underlying predicament, however, is that language is public, impossessible, indivisible (Komska and Moyd 2017). Not in the usual, false-pathos-filled meanings tied to the tired narratives of national unity or patriotism, but in the sense that it cannot be sliced into neat portions, artificially distilled, or otherwise separated for actual use. "Quoted speech" (literally, "another's speech") was the term that the famed Russian literary theorist Mikhail Bakhtin used to suggest that "we are dealing with someone else's words more often than with our own" (Pomorska 1984, p. ix). Whether we have a second-grade vocabulary or that of a latter-day Shakespeare, whether we are kleptocratic billionaires or fifth-generation rural poor, sharing at least some words, turns of phrase, grammatical constructions, and frames of reference is an inevitability particular to the medium of language. Such a destiny, of course, was not God-given but consciously chosen by our political ancestors, who went to great lengths to propagate an American idiom long before the high-speech digital traffic of news and social media came into play.

The echo-chamber approach—postulating that clear divisions exist and are easily reinforceable—may work for tracking how far opinions travel (or do not), but language consistently presents itself as a more complex and unpredictable ecology. There is "no natural property of language," chided the French philosopher Jacques Derrida those who would believe naively in the prospect of its wholesale appropriation or expropriation (Derrida 1998, p. 24). For better or worse, we are stuck with language being a shared resource, and we need to start treating it as such. This means not merely rinsing off, in the stream of our own prose and speech, the nouns, adjectives, and verbs after Trump had just claimed them for another early-morning tweet, but also critiquing, correcting, and caring for words that are never only our own.

And so, implicitly or (at times) explicitly, this book is also about Trump's words. And the neo-Nazi Andrew Anglin's words. And the words of Breitbart. And *The New York Times*. And Black Lives Matter activists. And Heather Heyer, who stood up against white nationalists and was killed for it in Charlottesville, VA, and her mother Susan Bro. And Bree Newsome, who scaled the flagpole outside the South Carolina Statehouse to take down a Confederate flag. And writers Zadie Smith and Jesmyn Ward and Colson Whitehead. Your grade-school teacher. Your car mechanic. Your uncle, the thought of seeing whom at a family get-together makes you cringe. The last sign language interpreter you encountered. Your refugee neighbor. Your pardon attorney. The expat you met backpacking in Ecuador. You. All of us.

A fair amount, although probably still not enough, has been said and written about linguistic obedience and disobedience in dictatorships and in oppressive, specifically colonial, settings. Conspicuous, by comparison, is the dearth of writing about linguistic obedience and disobedience in democracies. The classic oeuvres on civil disobedience, from Thoreau's 1849 "Resistance to Civil Government" to Howard Zinn's 1968 *Disobedience and Democracy* or even, for those who choose to be less America-centric, Leo Tolstoy's 1894 "On Patriotism" and related essays, do not accentuate language, even when individual words and languages come into the spotlight. As for the canon of civic obedience, dedicated to the shaping of dutiful citizens, much of it has continued to circle back to standard, monolingual speech.

"An Unfortunate Consequence of Democracy"

This is more than a little surprising, since linguistic disobedience and its uncomfortably facile slip into well-heeled obedience have been at the heart of reshaping language in democracy all along. Of this, American English used to be an indubitable paragon. The vernacular's very birth and eventual standardization in the long wake of the American Revolution are recorded as one protracted spell of linguistic disobedience, assisted and at times hampered by the zeal of the era's nationalist activist-philologists, such as Noah Webster or Benjamin Franklin. "Life is short, and every hour should be employed to good purposes," Webster wrote in his 1788 *On the Education of Young in America* (Webster n.d., p. 5). German, a serious competitor in the political arena, the less-than-"useful" Latin and Greek, and the "half-frivolous" French did not rank high on that list of vital priorities. British English, it went without saying, was the oppressive hegemon to be unseated with the help of spelling, lexicon, and grammar reforms. To champion American English was among the foundational acts of civic—indeed, democratic—rebellion.

The French sophisticate Alexis de Tocqueville knew to appreciate and fear the sweep of this emancipatory struggle, which raged on well into the twentieth century. Devoting an entire chapter of the 1835 *Democracy in America* to "How American Democracy has Modified the English Language," he observed with striking precision the porous membrane between linguistic obedience and disobedience.

In monarchies, he wrote, language is as though suspended in stasis. "Few new words are made, because few new things happen; and if you did new things, you would try hard to portray them with known words whose meaning has been fixed by tradition" (de Tocqueville 2012, p. 824). In democracies—the term that de Tocqueville kept using in plural but only in reference to the United States—smashing this smothering cast would seem like a liberating gesture. And in a sense it was, because suddenly people "communicate[d] constantly among themselves" (824). But this same exhilarating circumstance, it turns out, started off the pendular swings between linguistic disobedience and obedience that would later sustain the likes of Donald Trump. Democracy came bearing a verbal horn of plenty, but the gift was a Trojan horse: its citizens, while seemingly rebellious, "resembled each other more each day" (824).

In democracies, de Tocqueville explained, everything was in constant flux, and language had to keep up in a mad proto-Taylorist cycle. "The genius of democratic peoples," he reckoned, "shows itself not only in the great number of new words that they put into use, but also in the nature of the ideas that these new words represent" (823). Unbridled word coinage, he anticipated, was a creative but treacherous trap. America's amateur lexicographers entertained no serious etymological quests and, true to Webster's spirit, didn't care much for the classical tradition. Occasionally, some would pepper their speech with Greek or Latin, but that was only "ordinary vanity" and not actual erudition (824). There was, in fact, a correlation that de Tocqueville observed between the love of pompous vocabulary and the lacking understanding thereof. In short, Americans did not know what the fancy words meant but kept using them as garnishes, in any case.

Loads of utilitarian neologisms from living languages cropped up daily to reflect the "innovations," many on the spur of the moment. Not all were inspired to make up words from scratch. In many cases, America's verbal Golems were the retired clunky things of yore, which the users happily dusted off and endowed with several new lives at once. The fledgling not-quite-democracy ran on polysemy and tireless resignification before it ran on Dunkin', and the volumes ingested were comparable.

Knowledge wasn't necessary for the mass production of meaning, the startled de Tocqueville acknowledged, as "ignorance even facilitates" the expansion. Not surprisingly, the breakneck manufacture and consumption of verbiage came with their risks. "By doubling the meaning of a word" in the relentless whirl of physical movement and communication, he criticized, "democratic people make it doubtful which meaning they are leaving aside and which they are giving to it" (825). In each speaker's personal service and "with no permanent tribunal," words ran amok. A founder of sociolinguistics Einar Haugen would in the early 1970s dub America "a Babel in reverse" for its ability to swallow a myriad of tongues and regurgitate English only. In de Tocqueville's mind, something worse was afoot: the tower of Babel was American English itself. "This is an unfortunate consequence of democracy," he shuddered, imagining his native tongue. "I would prefer that you sprinkled the language with Chinese, Tartar or Huron words, than to make the meaning of French words uncertain. Harmony and homogeneity are only the secondary beauties of language" (825).

That ultimate rebellion, American English, if we were to heed the foreigner de Tocqueville, landed in a pile of wobbly sameness. That supreme act of linguistic disobedience, it turned out, begat linguistic obedience on a massive scale. Exactly this was the prophecy that Trump fulfilled on the steps of his event bus. It is also the prophecy with which all of us have yet to reckon as we re-envision language in a democracy and, paradoxical as this may sound, restore to it the power that it has never fully had.

Disobedience: Critique, Correction, Care in Language

If linguistic disobedience is not just a loud, inappropriate, flashy, utilitarian, mercantilist, and brash circumstance of democracy and if it isn't simply another obedient sheep in wolf's clothing—what is it? Redefined for today, we say, linguistic disobedience is refusing the spoils of interactional, communicative hegemony, in pursuit of something better. "Something better" remains a vague placeholder for now, but this is not to advertise yet another utopian mirage. Rather, the vagueness stipulates an open-ended set of terms that only an urgent and broad civic conversation about language in a democracy can hash out—the conversation that America and most other parts of the so-called Anglosphere have yet to have. These pages are kindling to that debate and not a blueprint—another top-down diktat, as it were—for what words to use or not.

"Crazy conservative fairy tales have become numbingly common," writes vox.com's David Roberts (2017), glossing his hypothesis that the United States in 2017 was facing an "epistemic crisis." An epistemic crisis is one in which time-honored paradigms of knowing, knowledge, and knowability appear to be failing. In international relations, too, the established narratives passed down from the Cold War era are disintegrating—though one wonders whether they even existed as coherent threads and not merely keyword assemblages in the first place (Pomerantsev 2018). Addressing narrative form and storytelling as they do, these claims are unavoidably also about language and its uses. What would it mean to say, along with Arjun Appadurai (2016) and others, that the United States and other self-styled modern democracies are currently encountering a linguistic crisis? In lieu of debating whether "crisis" is an overused explanatory device, we suggest turning attention rather to the nature of language as something in contemporary democratic life that finds itself under particular strain, fracture, and, let's be honest, neglect.

A book written in English is perhaps not the most germane venue for making this point. But at least we can point out some structural features that plague the very ways in which we tend to think (or not think) about language. The German literary theorist Robert Stockhammer (2017) recently called attention to the fact that English is predestined, by its own lexical limitations, to remain unattentive to two different conceptions of language, easily recognized as different in, say, French but much harder to convey in the aforesaid pair "idiom" and "language." Stockhammer explains the very salient, very consequential difference in French between *langue* and *langage,* by way of a kind of translingual rule-of-thumb:

> Looking more closely at Anglophone usage affords us a quick way of testing the difference (though not an entirely disambiguating translation of it): if tongue can replace the word language in a certain context, it refers to the concept of langue. If this substitution is not possible, one is dealing with a langage. This conforms to the etymological substrate, in the sense that both the English tongue and the French langue also denote a language organ

(though in langage the suffix –age neutralizes this etymologic connection). (Stockhammer 2017, p. 34)

Why and when does this matter? Philosophical reflections on language, let's say, Richard Rorty's and Ludwig Wittgenstein's, "rarely reflected on the fact that nearly all of [their] examples stemmed from one singular language" (Stockhammer 2017, p. 34). Similarly, in the Trump era, media profiles of writers and thinkers who issued dire warnings about the spread of authoritarianism, from Orwell to Karl Popper, tend to tout transparent language as the unproblematic and uniformly desirable ideal. If such critiques sound out language as a universal human faculty (i.e., the French *langage*), they are going to have great difficulty reflecting at the same time on how discrete, national, standardized languages (i.e., *langues*) impose particular historical limitations on language use. The conflation of *langue* and *langage* in reflection on language (for example, in English or German, where the lexical distinction does not effectively exist) means that ambiguity and imprecision will tend to rule the roost when it comes to thinking and thinking well about language in contemporary life. This can only compound the imprecision that already exists within each tongue, of which de Tocqueville offered us but a singular preview.

So when we approach language as a central feature of a civic crisis—of a moment of grave danger and unspeakable suffering for many whose very lives and livelihoods are directly affected—we need to be able to bridge this conceptual divide. When we speak of language, it is not just standard and neoliberally shiny UK Standard English, Colombian Spanish, French, Ewe, Mandarin, Scots, Moroccan Arabic, or Slovak that we mean. These *langues* are historical products, complex perlocutionary effects of imperial/colonial and postimperial/postcolonial nation-building. They are deeply meaningful to their speakers and to those who worked, often their entire lives, to produce and care for them. But these *langues* are increasingly subject to practices that, as the Africanist sociolinguist Sinfree Makoni and the Australian applied linguist Alastair Pennycook (2006) demonstrate, tend to disinvent and reconstitute those *langues* into something that is no longer a *langue* but, perhaps a *langage*—an idiom that knows no stable, reproducible position within the world language hierarchy.

One of the terms researchers have used to account for these everyday linguistic acts in which people engage, unwittingly or strategically, to disinvent and reconstitute language from *langue* to *langage* is "translanguaging." In the context of his discussion of New Chinglish, Li Wei (2016, p. 4) describes the practice of translanguaging as "using one's idiolect or linguistic repertoire without regard for socially and politically defined language labels or boundaries—in order to make sense, solve problems, articulate one's thought, and gain knowledge." In a sense, de Tocqueville's image of American English—the "language of a democracy"—has become an itinerant template of translanguaging, unhinged from any specific social order and, as we will see momentarily, physical space. Such practices are usually disregarded by systemic reflections on language, and thus also by polemics about monolingualism, because the translanguaging impulse does not even necessarily grant that *langues* exist, in any more real way than do any other metaphysical constructions. Unlike the notion of "code-switching," that is, alternating between two languages or more, translanguaging "questions the proposition that what bilinguals are doing is going from one language to another" (García and Lin 2016, p. 3). Such linguistically disobedient practices therefore build the possibility of a space, a translanguaging space, which "breaks down the artificial dichotomies between the macro and the micro, the societal and the individual, and the social and the psycho" (Li Wei 2011, p. 1234).

It is important to note at this point that such a notion, which highlights practices that undermine the historical, empirical, and explanatory validity of *langues*/individual languages, faces a great deal of resistance, precisely in a twenty-first century that has found ways to monetize standardized languages. Katznelson and Bernstein (2017) show how "bilingual education" of the 1980s and 1990s, coded as bound to heritage and ethnicity, has been rebranded for the new century as "multilingual competence," where acquiring and mastering individual languages are seen as central to professional and commercial success. Though it may indeed show complex features of "neoliberalism from below" (Gago 2014), translanguaging practices have not meaningfully registered in the international regime of "reactionary multilingualism" (Moore 2015). They have remained an inconvenient-seeming but much needed opposition.

One of the things Donald Trump has done so effectively—in ways that his surrogates and press secretaries routinely and fascinatingly fail at—is to perform the prerogative, the very public prerogative, of having a distinctive idiom, a *langage*. Though he will certainly pander to those who purport to protect the American English *langue* from outsiders, he luxuriously spreads out into interactional territory from which centuries of linguistic theory have barred the rest of us: that of the messy, unrationalized idiolect. All while professing monolingualism—and letting his multilingual spokespeople preach it on his behalf ("He speaks English. That's it. And that's okay," Melania Trump told *Harper's Bazaar* in 2016)—Trump has helped himself to the extreme opposite. His behavior falls within the purview of what scholars like Jane Hill, Scott Kiesling, Jonathan Rosa, and Nelson Flores identify as the structural privilege of cisgender male "white linguistic disorder," when immigrants, queer people, and people of color are subjected to aggressive verbal hygiene throughout their lives by institutions and individuals alike. What Trump has tantalizingly done—among other things, and like many other demagogues in recent and less than recent history—is to elevate *langage* to a tool of interactional hegemony.

By interactional hegemony, we mean the deliberate or unwitting use of a reliably effective set of linguistic tools to "win the hand" in face-to-face, real-time, naturally occurring talk, or its simulations on Twitter, social media, and in other contexts. These linguistic tools often come from a complex and exclusive proprietary template that combines obedient and disobedient styles. Rationalists hasten to point out ways in which this man, this Trump, comes off to onlookers as clueless and out-of-touch in interaction after interaction, and therefore draw the comfortable conclusion that he has *lost* face or power in such interactions. In doubling down into such analytic arm-chair quarterbacking of interaction, rationalists imagine a paradise of language in which points are being tallied over the long arc of history, karma is being amassed, and the fragility of this, or any, dotty patriarch's idiom is becoming ever more visible. The emperor, many are eager to scream, has no clothes. This kind of credulity, however, betrays an obedience to the scientistic and analytical laurels upon which verbal hygienists (Cameron 1995) have rested since the nineteenth century. That era's so-called Young Grammarians, befuddled by the individual speaker's unpredictable liveliness, "emphasized the impersonal rule-governed aspect of language because it permitted them to make claims that were more general and abstract, similar to those of natural scientists, who were attempting to understand the laws of physics" (Holquist 2014, p. 11). Agency, by this token, became an expendable variable.

Such a scientistic, morphological orientation to language was deeply invested in reproducing the normative category of *langue* in each new civic context. This set of stances and habits endured deep into the post-colonial language planning projects of the 1960s and 1970s, when the ideal "modern" language needed to be a fully fledged, orderly, rational *langue* (Ricento 2000). As multilingualisms from below begin to undo the explanatory power of *langue* (the rational, systemic unity of "a" language), a battle of *langages* is ensuing between demagogues' idiolects and translanguagers' instincts. The quest for agency is written all over it.

For the purposes of this book then, linguistic obedience is also always also an obedience to so-called linguistic monism. Like monism's philosophical brands, linguistic monism (from the Greek μόνος, lone or solitary) is a positive belief system that "conceives the world as consisting of geographically dispersed common languages each of which has a unique separate identity of its own that is both stable and unitary. In its aspect as an ideology of denial, monism thus opposes the reality of change; each of the distinct common languages it recognizes as a solid entity is of course at an unstable point in its history as a system" (Holquist 2014, p. 8). Disobedience in language(s) is, from this viewpoint, an unwillingness to cash in on the complex and ubiquitous privileges of monolingualism, and instead to engage in practices that imagine the world not as a federation of distinct language-states, but as a dynamic and interwoven ecology of languages always becoming one another, changing one another, discovering one another.

We, Authors and Readers

As we mention in the opening, writing *Linguistic Disobedience* was not part of our personal or professional plans until after the 2016 US General Election. Among the urgent and important messages the election results conveyed to us was that honest, collaborative, and courageous work on the questions of our civic moment must take precedence over our traditional arenas of expertise. We did not write this book because we felt uniquely competent to do so, but because we could and we wanted to. Each of us is a mid-career tenured professor at a research university, and each of us enjoys an extraordinarily privileged status in the relations of power that surround us—despite having lived a life-long experience of the queer, the person of color, the woman, the differently abled, the immigrant. In the collaborative spirit that enabled this book to emerge, we have chosen to write "as one and as multiple," weaving in and out of first-person singular and plural enunciation as best befits the respective moment. The chapters convey a breadth of linguistic styles and authorial tones to show that conversations about civic language do not mandate speaking in the same key, that they do not have to succumb to editorial or stylistic monism. We each consider ourselves responsible for the entirety of the book, and we each look forward to discussing it, sharing it, and accounting for it in our future work as scholars, activists, teachers, and learners.

For whom is this book? As every audience-related question, this one is a thicket and may not be worth the speculation at all. Starting out, we wrote for ourselves, because the process of co-authoring—in awe of the others' knowledge, in gratitude for their intellectual and emotional generosity, and in the consciousness of their critical eye—makes small mental universes collide and expand, or dissipate for lack of resonance beyond our solitary rumination. As we brainstormed changing minds about language, ours were the first to change. That means the effort has paid off. But of course, the three of us could have achieved a similar result without committing time and energy to writing a book. Naturally, some greater ambition must have sustained our urge to put pen to paper, or fingertips to keyboard. The dream challenge would be to reach out to those who don't believe that language (be it as *langue* or *langage*) matters, or to those who categorically refuse to read others or to listen to them, whoever those "others" may be. However, we are well aware of how arrogantly utopian cherishing such a hope would be for a book that, already due to the topic, cannot possibly pretend to be non-partisan. For this reason, we wrote with an eye to those who already have a soft spot for language, as fledgling or sophisticated readers, writers, musicians, artists, language-learners, politicians, or activists—to our still-unknown inspirations, co-conspirators, critics—in the hope that they will read, consider in silence, correct, talk back, care.

Notes

1. The phrase "linguistic disobedience" served as the focal point for a series of poems by the Australian poet John Kinsella, in his collection *Peripheral Light*.

References

Appadurai, Arjun. *Banking on Words: The Failure of Language in the Age of Derivative Finance*. Chicago: The University of Chicago Press, 2016.

Bourdieu, Pierre. *The Field of Cultural Production*. Translated and edited by Randal Johnson. New York: Columbia University Press, 1993.

Cameron, Deborah. *Verbal Hygiene*. London: Verso, 1995.

Chen, Adrian. "The Agency." *The New York Times*, June 2, 2015.

Clark, Alex. "Breitbart's Boyle: Our Goal Is the 'Elimination of the Entire Mainstream Media.'" *Breitbart.com*, July 19, 2017.

De Tocqueville, Alexis. *Democracy in America*. Translated by James T. Schleifer. Indianapolis: Liberty Fund, 2012.

Derrida, Jacques. *Monolingualism of the Other: or, the Prosthesis of Origin*. Translated by Patrick Mensah. Stanford: Stanford University Press, 1998.

Didion, Joan. *Slouching Towards Bethlehem*. New York: Farrar, Straus and Giroux, 2008.

Gago, Veronica. *Neoliberalism from Below: Popular Pragmatics and Baroque Economies*. Translated by Liz Mason-Reese. Durham: Duke University Press, 2014.

García, Ofelia and Angel M.Y. Lin. "Translanguaging in Bilingual Education." In *Bilingual and Multilingual Education (Encyclopedia of Language and Education)*, edited by Ofelia García, Angel Lin, and Stephan May. New York: Springer, 2016.

Green, David. "A Call to Linguistic Disobedience." *The American Interest*, July 10, 2012. https://www.the-american-interest.com/2012/06/10/a-call-to-linguistic-disobedience/.

Havel, Václav. *The Power of the Powerless: Citizens Against the State in Central-Eastern Europe*, edited by John Keane and translated by Paul Wilson. Armonk, NY: M. E. Sharpe, 1985.

Hill, Jane H. "Mock Spanish: A Site for the Indexical Reproduction of Racism in American English." *Language & Culture, Symposium* 2 (1995). http://language-culture.binghamton.edu/symposia/2/part1/index.html.

Holquist, Michael. "What Would Bakhtin Do?" *Critical Multilingualism Studies* 2, no. 1 (2014): 6–19.

Katznelson, Noah and Katie Bernstein. "Rebranding Bilingualism: The Shifting Discourses of Language Education Policy in California's 2016 Election." *Linguistics and Education* 40 (2017): 11–26.

Kinsella, John. *Peripheral Light*. New York: W. W. Norton, 2005.

Komska, Yuliya and Michelle Moyd. "Language Is a Public Thing." *Lateral* 6, no. 2 (2017). http://csalateral.org/issue/6-2/language-public-thing-komska-moyd/.

Li Wei. "Moment Analysis and Translanguaging Space: Discursive Construction of Identities by Multilingual Chinese Youth in Britain." *Journal of Pragmatics* 43 (2011): 1222–35.

Li Wei. "New Chinglish and the Post-Multilingualism Challenge: Translanguaging ELF in China." *Journal of English as a Lingua Franca* 5, no. 1 (2016): 1–25.

Loseff, Lev. *On the Beneficence of Censorship: Aesopian Language in Modern Russian Literature.* Munich: Otto Sagner, 1984.

Makoni, Sinfree and Alastair Pennycook. *Disinventing and Reconstituting Languages.* Bristol: Multilingual Matters, 2006.

Makoni, Sinfree, Geneva Smitherman, Arnetha F. Ball, and Arthur K. Spears. "Toward Black Linguistics." In *Black Linguistics: Language, Society, and Politics in Africa and the Americas,* edited by Arnetha F. Ball, Geneva Smitherman, and Sinfree Makoni. London: Routledge, 2003.

Marx, Karl. *The Eighteenth Brumaire of Louis Bonaparte.* Translated by Daniel De Leon. London: Electric Books, 2001.

McWhorter, John. *Talking Back, Talking Black: Truths About America's Lingua Franca.* New York: Bellevue Literary Press, 2016.

Moore, Robert. "From Revolutionary Monolingualism to Reactionary Multilingualism: Top-Down Discourses of Linguistic Diversity in Europe, 1794–Present." *Language and Communication* 44 (2015): 19–30.

Moyd, Michelle and Yuliya Komska. "Donald Trump Is Changing Our Language. We Need a Language of Resistance." *The Guardian,* January 17, 2017. https://www.theguardian.com/commentisfree/2017/jan/17/resist-donald-trump-vocabulary-resistance-rhetoric.

Pell, Nicholas. "6 Things You Learn Getting Paid to Troll People Online." *Cracked.com,* May 27, 2015. http://www.cracked.com/blog/6-things-you-learn-getting-paid-to-troll-people-online/.

Pomerantsev, Peter. "Jokes and the Death of Narratives." *The American Interest,* March 24, 2018. https://www.the-american-interest.com/2018/03/24/jokes-death-narratives/.

Pomorska, Krystyna. Foreword to Mikhail Bakhtin, *Rabelais and His World.* Translated by Helene Iswolsky. Bloomington: Indiana University Press, 1984.

Ricento, Thomas. "Historical and Theoretical Perspectives in Language Policy and Planning." *Journal of Sociolinguistics* 4, no. 2 (2000): 196–213.

Roberts, David. "America Is Facing an Epistemic Crisis." *Vox.com*, November 2, 2017. https://www.vox.com/policy-and-politics/2017/11/2/16588964/america-epistemic-crisis.

Scott, James C. *Domination and the Arts of Resistance: Hidden Transcripts*. New Haven: Yale University Press, 1990.

Stockhammer, Robert. "Converting Lingualism into Linguality (*langagification des langues*) in Goethe's Wilhelm Meister Novels." Translated by Judith Menzl. *Critical Multilingualism Studies* 5, no. 3 (2017): 32–51.

Summers, Lawrence. "What You (Really) Need to Know." *The New York Times*, January 20, 2012. http://www.nytimes.com/2012/01/22/education/edlife/the-21st-century-education.html.

Tannen, Deborah. "New York Jewish Conversational Style." *International Journal of the Sociology of Language* 30 (1981): 133–149.

Webster, Noah. *On the Education of Youth in America*. The Federalist Papers Project. https://www.commonlit.org/texts/on-the-education-of-youth-in-america.

2

Critique

Though of classical Greek origin, critique in its modern visage has had a bit of a French flair. The word rhymes with mystique and with the names of ravishing adventure-novel heroines. But hold the boudoir clichés and any hope for silky elegance, supple wit, or erotic intimacy. Unlike the other two practices this book advances in the name of nurturing linguistic disobedience—correction and care—critique stubbornly refuses to do its work gently. It is no coincidence that philosopher and sociologist Bruno Latour likens critique to a sledgehammer. With it, he swoons ever so slightly, "you can do a lot of things: break down walls, destroy idols, ridicule prejudices, but you cannot repair, take care, assemble, reassemble, stitch together" (Latour 2010, p. 475). Punitive, arrogant, authoritarian, and vitriolic are critique's common epithets (Felski 2015).

Long before Latour's sledgehammer image, "police" had been the Enlightenment-era analogy of choice for "critique," which was coming into its own as a genre of thought. The rise of something as apparently negative, restrictive, and disciplining called for a vindication. Critique's overreach seemed obvious to its detractors. But, as philosopher Immanuel Kant notes in the preface to the second edition of *Critique of Pure Reason* (1781), it is not without advantages. Critique, he insists, removes obstacles on the path toward the practical use of whatever

© The Author(s) 2019
Y. Komska et al., *Linguistic Disobedience*,
https://doi.org/10.1007/978-3-319-92010-8_2

its object may be, allowing liberation, growth, and action to ensue. "To deny that this service rendered by [...] critique has a positive benefit," Kant advocates, "would be like saying that the police provides no positive benefit" (Kant 1996, p. 27).

With "police brutality" and "police shootings" saturating the head-lines, the positive benefits of policing can be a tough sell in the twenty-first century. This spectrum of formulations includes also "language police," the widespread cipher for unsolicited encroachment upon the freedom of speech, dictating not only what to say but how. Has critique outlived its purpose? Has it turned into a liability more than an asset? Doesn't its "long history of legislation, prohibition and interdiction" fos-ter obedience rather than the opposite (Felski 2015)? Each time, it is tempting to answer in the affirmative.

But what about language critique—the kind of critique that trains us to respond to "language change in the age of technology" (Gilbert 1971, p. 987)? To probe the relationship between language and reality. To "reduce the manipulation of language by advertisers, slogan makers, jour-nalists, politicians so as to promote the freedom of the individual" (Gauger 1995, p. 41). To think about more than just select words—over-used, abused, lacking, banned, lost, quaint—as we too often do, but rather to attend to language in its entirety. To notice the buildup of lop-sided interactional advantages, the crimes of unjust appropriation, the biases of unequal recognition. Also, to see the beauty and tenacity that bind language to joy and affirmation, rather than only to ailment and extinction.

This kind of critique is more than a power tool or a police force. Where the skeptics suspect authoritarianism or elitism, the adepts see "intransi-gent opposition to the status quo," rigor, historical watchfulness, and a readiness to expose "omissions, contradictions, insufficiencies, or eva-sions" (Felski 2015). The famed theorist Michel Foucault's definition of it was the "art of voluntary insubordination" (Foucault 2002, p. 194). Much closer to disobedience, this vision of critique deserves another chance—if not a profound revival—as we approach the third decade of the twenty-first century.

With an eye to language, then, the critical agent would be not a cop but a different sort of sleuth altogether: the "language detective," armed with little more than alertness, acuity of perception, and an analytical mind. The vocation has indeed received surprising attention lately. Some insist that the language detectives should remain a small, even elite guild. This, so the argument goes, is because the role takes "a particular sort of human," a person who is "between a linguistics academic, an archival historian, a journalist and an old-fashioned gumshoe" (Dickson 2018). Others, helmed by the writer Rebecca Solnit, understand the job to be considerably more democratic. "We all are language detectives," she writes, "going out into the world and looking for all the unhallowed speech of political statements and news headlines," because "it is the truest, highest purpose of language to make things clear and help us see" (Solnit 2016).

Are we really all so engaged? It is indeed a wisdom as old as Confucius that rectifying names (that is, words) to align them with the world is a foundational activity of human life. But in today's Anglosphere, defined though it may be by its (English) tongue, language is at the very bottom of the priorities list. If the German classic Johann Wolfgang von Goethe (1749–1832) once grumbled that "every person believes, because he speaks, that he can speak about language" (1978, p. 511),[1] today's grumble seems to be that everyone can speak without speaking about language at all. The token chant *language matters* remains popular in certain quarters. Living up to the notion is much less so. This makes two things clear about the future of language critique and the role of prospective so-called language detectives in it.

One, a small group will not suffice. Outsourcing language-critical habits to a small sliver of the population has been a long-established rule. Historically—already George Orwell noted this—we owe the righting of linguistic wrongs not to "any automated evolutionary process but [...] to the conscious action of a minority" (Orwell 1968, p. 138). In the long run, though, it seems that no minority can bear exclusive responsibility for the wear and tear that the majority causes to a shared resource.

This is especially important because those who have been overburdened in this regard include not only the "minority" of language professionals or white journalists whom Orwell likely had in mind, but actual minorities, ethnic, racial, sexual, and persons with disabilities. Exactly those whose purported language deficits or "quirks" have rendered them suspect or inefficient in the eyes of the intolerant. The example of the industrialist Henry Ford is memorable. With the brutal efficiency that his name conjures, he recruited unpaid volunteers to teach English to thousands of immigrant workers at his factories in order to optimize production. In the same minority are also those who have pushed for more inclusive vocabularies, often in isolation, and even when their pleas fell on deaf ears. And those who have found they must resort to a foreign language to count as human: Angela Davis recalls how only switching to French allowed her personhood to be acknowledged in the Jim Crow South (Kaplan 2012, p. 149). Such people's linguistic consciousness amounts to the ultimate, and unappreciated, form of language loyalty. Not the rah-rah-patriotic devotion to a specific vernacular but an enduring commitment to language as a cause deserving of its own kind of vigilance. For much too long, this has been an unshared burden. With language, as Pierre Bourdieu writes, there is no "trickle-down effect" (1991, p. 64), no pars-pro-toto repair.

This expanded cohort of language detectives would persevere, however, not merely in the interest of monolingualism. The political right-versus-left rifts that English has recently experienced—in the absence of a "shared moral language" or even a shared reality to reference—reveal that speaking the same tongue is no guarantee of civic cohesion, even though integration zealots in the United States and the United Kingdom preach otherwise (Blankenhorn 2018; Gessen 2017a; Karatsareas 2018). The solution is not forcible integration into a single language community but scrutiny and reform of the political forces, from school curricula to election campaigns, that shape some speakers into entitled and xenophobic purveyors of phantom loyalties and others into overworked life-long guardians of tongues native and adopted.

Language, more people must recognize, is an everyday exercise of power rather than a closed system of arcane rules (Bourdieu 1991, p. 45). How that power gets distributed matters. The promotion of one tongue or norm regularly occurs at the cost of diminishing or suppressing others. If, in response, language itself turns into a "war zone," as the Kenyan writer Ngũgĩ wa Thiong'o suggests it does, it is a war that pushes back against hegemony, that hashes out a cohesion premised on equitability and not on prescribed consensus. In those moments, language detectives are called up as "language warriors" to champion languages in the plural

(Dyussu 2017). Lending this task particular urgency is the fact that multilingualism is on its way to becoming a hallmark of social media bots rather than of actual people (Confessore et al. 2018), and that most present-day Anglophone defenders of language act as though linguistic monism were the norm.

Had we all been language detectives all along, we would have routinely exposed and opposed some of the most far-reaching and baneful social and political transformations which language has aided and abetted lately. We would have noticed, for example, how the proliferation of harmless-looking monikers, such as "curator" or "pivot," is quietly shaping diverse institutions in a single corporate image (Gardner 2013; Silverman 2017). We would have foreseen that the verb "weaponize," in its unbridled gallop across screens and pages, is failing to diffuse militancy and channel pacifism (Kelly 2016). Contrary to such intuitive delusions, "weaponize" is now a favorite among National Rifle Association spokespeople, who use it against their unarmed critics (Reston 2017). Were we all active, veteran language sleuths, we would have insisted that it is impossible to criticize the CIA for its torture practices while continuing to call them, euphemistically, "enhanced interrogation." We would have insisted on clearer definitions for such "linguistic omnivore" terms as "neoliberalism" sooner, before they are dismissed out of hand as fuzzy and lacking "discriminatory power" (Rogers 2018; Bourdieu 1991, p. 64).

We would have also balked at the worldwide diffusion of Trumpisms—not amplifying, even in parody, its range of words, devised as destructive missiles (Moyd and Komska 2017; Lakoff 2018). We would have nipped the label "fake news" in the bud, to name an example, well before the recommendation of the European Commission's High Level Expert Group needed to do so in March 2018 (European Commission 2018). Our protest pending and irresolute, the incumbent American president's pet expression had seeped as far as Myanmar. There, within months, officials conscripted it to the goals of erasing a real people, the Rohingya, from history and place (Beech 2017).

We would have rejected Donald Trump's addiction to capital letters not simply because it carries an incongruent Elizabethan ring, but because capitalization hollows out meaning, turning words into mottos and mottos into jabs. "When a word is properly defined," philosopher

Simone Weil wrote in 1937, "it loses its capital letter and can no longer serve as a banner or a hostile slogan; it becomes simply a sign, helping us grasp some concrete reality" (Weil 1962, p. 156). We would have noticed that some leading global publications, in this crucial moment, are discontinuing their language blogs—"Mind Your Language" at *The Guardian*, "On Language" at *The New York Times*, "Lexicon Valley" at *Slate* (now only a podcast)—or that the blogs still in existence, such as "Word on the Street" at *Wall Street Journal* or "Lingua Franca" at the *Chronicle of Higher Education*, often lose sight of the big civic picture amid the amusing lexicographic quirks.

We would have considered devising counterlanguages—sets of oppositional conventions and practices with which to reclaim disobedience from the powers that, as we have outlined in the introduction, had moved to usurp it. Counterlanguage isn't an unfamiliar notion in the age of the authoritarians, when examples from other countries that routinely censor public language keep pouring in. From Russia, we hear about the perseverance of underground slang, *mat*, illicit under czarist rule, then outlawed in the Soviet Union, and now again banned by Vladimir Putin (Remnik 2014). Chinese examples have been too many to count, capitalizing on the polysemy of spoken words and phrases, logograms, and the allusions they can convey when aided by the lightning speed of social media (Si 2017). Why wait for censorship?

In greater numbers, we would have also registered all the good that language can bring—contact, communication, knowledge, the beauty of the word sung, written, or expressed in a gesture—the true reasons why preserving it is worth the effort.

Many, maybe even most of us, have not done that. If we had, the periodic fear that those in power can "take all the words" (Gessen 2017b) or "monopolize the public transcript" (Scott 1990, p. 54) would be less insidious. Solnit's optimistic assessment turns out to be more aspirational than factual. We have yet to *become* language detectives (Gessen 2017a). The purpose would be not only to "create the conditions for the formerly silenced to speak and be heard" (Solnit 2017, p. 21), but also to compel those who have long enjoyed both of these privileges to realize that their speech is not unconditional, whatever the constitutional freedoms. Instead of using language as a form of entitlement, we must all learn to scrutinize it more honestly, coolly, and constantly—and fight for the language and languages that we want.

But Solnit is right in her sense that the story of language is too often told in bleak tones, as one of control or ambush. Much more has been written about Newspeak-like invasions than about techniques for averting or rebuffing them, or for raising a queer, colorful, and righteous ruckus that is louder than Newspeak itself. Such techniques have long been in existence, despite being scattered across periods and places and communities of practice. They date back much further than Orwell's famed essay "Politics and the English Language." This chapter aims to recover their formal cornerstone—critique—and taps into critique's methods by outlining its more than century-long contemporary history.

We hope the excursion will offer some useful lessons and suggestions. But more likely, it will reveal that formulating clandestine prescriptions or issuing recipes—the conceit, as we spell in the introduction, of many past thinkers about disobedience—is a futile and presumptive endeavor. The point of fostering linguistic disobedience is not to hand down answers to Vladimir Lenin's proverbial "What is to be done?" but rather to invite you to think: "What can I do?" Such introspection can best begin with and in silence.

Silence

Nearing the end of his life, the saturnine modernist James Joyce developed a literary habit that may seem exploitative to some, communal to others. Long poor of eyesight—so much so that his daughter Lucia was named for the medieval patron saint of the blind—Joyce would ask fellow writers to read and summarize books for him. Samuel Beckett, a future classic in his own right, found himself pulled into the master's "notesnatching operation" or, in the eye of a less involved and thus more forgiving beholder, his homespun republic of letters (Ben-Zvi 1982, p. 143).

His fellow-sufferers were luckier, left to leaf through Mark Twain's *Huckleberry Finn* or Victorian mystery novels (Van Hulle 2005, p. 53). Beckett's draw was heavy fare: Fritz Mauthner's *Beiträge zu einer Kritik der Sprache* (*Contributions to a Critique of Language*) in the original

German. Since described as an anthology of "passionate, rambling vituperations, contradictions, and logorrhea" and untranslated into English to this day, the hefty three-volume oeuvre had originally appeared between 1901 and 1902 and went through three printings by 1923 (Ben-Zvi 1980, pp. 183–184). A bestseller it was not, by any conventional yardstick. But its energies did hit the era's nerve, agitated as it would have already been by a revaluation of just about anything, from political ideologies to the arts.

Of course, a host of notoriously prolific Germanophone thinkers such as Johann Gottfried Herder (1744–1803), Friedrich Schlegel (1772–1829), or Wilhelm von Humboldt (1767–1835)—to say nothing of others, such as John Locke (1632–1704) or Giambattista Vico (1668–1744)—had spilled ink on language long before Mauthner (1849–1923). Many of those earlier obsessions, however, had treated their object—and here comes Mauthner's pet peeve—as something peripheral to the expression of ideas. Swooning over language family trees, over the role of language in human history, even over the obscurest of consonant shifts, stem changes, and dialectal variants had rendered thinkers blind to the words dripping off their own quill and pen tips. Didn't language, Mauthner energetically objected, amount to more than the sum of its pasts?

Accounts differ as to the year when Beckett first ventured into the *Contributions'* leather-corseted depths. Some date the encounter back to 1937, following the writer's return from a six-month-long junket across Nazi Germany and his wrestling match with the "grand, old, plastic words" of the German tongue, in the country that had already started to warp them.[2] Beckett himself recalls having reckoned with Mauthner much earlier, around 1929 or 1930. Whatever the case, the writer digested the treatise and made sprawling notes. The ideas stuck, and half a century on, he relayed their gist in three punchy, unpunctuated lines. "For me," Beckett shared,

> it came down to:
> Thought words
> Words inane
> Thought inane. (Ben-Zvi 1984, p. 66)

This gloss of what was the first self-professed, stand-alone, multi-volume critique of language was laconic, if not comprehensive. Language was alpha and omega—the beginning of things and, sadly, a harbinger of their own decline. True, our present day may boast "an unparalleled, still unfolding and uncertain transformation of public language," as writes the journalist Mark Thompson, a transformation arising from years of neglect (2016, p. 2). But Mauthner's age made a similar wager about its own turbulent relationship to language and reality. Rumors of a looming civilizational decline murmured in the background, as they usually do on such occasions, though in 1901 no obvious political cataclysm was rattling the language edifice yet. In Mauthner's view, no such tipping point was required—a useful reminder for today's language detectives.

Beloved and maligned, the turn of the century was for the critic yet another nightmarish recurrence of Rome *redivivus*. The West was crumbling, and its language was a sign of the downfall. Just as Latin had hiccupped to presage ancient Rome's erosion, the modern languages of Europe, as far as Mauthner could see, had rotted under the golden burnish of the Belle Époque. Still, he rushed to contradict himself: language was not only an early victim in society's suicide, but also a weapon. Words padded the era's obsessions with sensual comforts, upheld bromidic metaphors, dangled as fetishes atop the otherwise threadbare literary wardrobes, hampered the progress of science, and loomed as the golden calf to which the superstitious prayed when all else seemed lost. The problem wasn't so much a particular crisis as it was language itself—an untrustworthy ally, as Mauthner's baroque invectives put it. Resisting the siren call of "word hunger," time was ripe to "learn to be silent again," he declared (1901, p. 2, 215). Only how?

Choice

A language detective can aim high, at the crimes that bear names in need of parenthetical explanation: semanticide (perversion of meaning), verbal anarchy ("mudslinging, emotionalism, and debasement of words"), xenologophobia (purism), xenologophilia (excessive attachment to foreign borrowings) (Wesley Young 1991, pp. 105, 25, 81). Or drop the scholastic pretenses and focus on euphemisms, pathos, jargon, name-calling, on the gaps in the existing vocabularies where variegated human misdemeanors, from sexual violence to disdain for nature, are concerned (Grady 2017; Monbiot 2017). Or consider all other words we lack. Or simply think of what *could* be said: spot that abandoned megaphone on the sidewalk and behold the dust that it has gathered, well before bending down to pick it up, and certainly before letting it project voice.

Easier said than done. The rush to speak and bolster messages is overwhelming. And overrated. The tongue—the embodied reality of most languages, in which writers on-the-hyphen delight for its raw fleshiness—babbles, boneless, in one's mouth. The act of moving the tongue is not in itself praiseworthy. "Twist it in any direction and it will turn that way," the Turkish-German writer Emine Sevgi Özdamar warns of the muscle's unpredictably wide ambling range (1994, p. 9). For those who do not live in dictatorships, speaking is often easier than thinking about speaking. Speech—free speech, especially—occupies a prominent place in the civic imagination. People fight over and for it. Pondering speech, broadly defined, is another matter.

In the guise of language critique, thinking about language—practically and profoundly—remains uncharted territory in many democracies. There is no tribute to it in the pantheon of civic virtues, no campaign waged to extend to it any special protections, no pageantry to celebrate its benefits. On the contrary, thinking before speaking is being increasingly tied to (self-)censorship or securitization of language. It is the likes of the Pentagon's counterinsurgency manuals that instruct subordinates to "consider what they wish to say" first (Rafael 2016, pp. 139–141). Civilian language how-tos remain mute on the topic. According to its critics, the military's strategic silence-before-speech imperative fosters a language that is transparent, devoid of its usual "noise," de-individualized, and thus easily malleable by those in charge as a kind of government property. True this well may be, although many of the modern age's writing gurus, from Orwell to lexicographer Henry Watson Fowler, the man behind the *Concise Oxford English Dictionary*, advocated a similarly plain style—to many a glowing review. By overlooking these uneasy parallels between civic and martial ideals around language pragmatism and, in the same breath, leaving the military with an industrial monopoly on thinking before speaking—that prudent moment of intelligent silence—we surrender our agency.

There are exceptions. Writer Robert Macfarlane (2015) and lexicographer Susie Dent (2016) prove Orwell short-sighted on the importance of "salvaging [...] obsolete words and turns of speech" (1968, p. 138). They gather endangered, vanishing words to prevent entire physical and poetic—local and regional—worlds from being erased in our stupefied acquiescence. Their work has hit a nerve, bolstering the language detectives' ranks. Thousands now follow them on social media, retrieving forgotten words across languages day by day. Others, like journalist Mark Thompson, advocate for a full-on recovery of the art of rhetoric to register its persistent abuses (2016). Historians such as Timothy Snyder admonish us to "be kind to our language" (2017, pp. 60–64). But do these individual routines add up to an adequate regimen, a vocation of contemporary language intelligence?

They do. Language critique—as Mauthner's brainchild has been properly known among journalists, philosophers, writers, and linguists outside the Anglosphere—is that regimen. Its history reveals that minding language neither presumes extreme circumstances nor warrants deep scholasticism. Authoritarian or totalitarian regimes needn't be standing on our doorstep, although confrontations with them do act as sure catalysts. Professional linguists needn't mastermind the pushback; in fact, some of them have discounted language critique itself as too unscientific. Critical language consciousness has been, from its cradle in the early twentieth century, a public impulse. It can and should thrive in the most ordinary of times, cultivating the trifecta of these everyday habits: *distrust, disinterestedness*, and *distance*. Neither costly nor utopian, these three direct our ample propensity for suspicion away from conspiracy theories, doomsday rumors, and personal grudges—and toward wiser uses.

Their low cost notwithstanding, few have coveted the "three Ds". History buffs might balk at the echo of the occupying Allies' disciplining vision for Germany after Hitler, encapsulated then in the "five Ds": denazification, demilitarization, democratization, decentralization, decartelization. This association is not entirely off the mark. Like those policies, choosing language critique presumes a conscious change of mind. At the same time, the analogy could be better. Distance, distrust, and disinterestedness are no Latinate byproducts ending in "-tion," imposed from the top down by foreigners and therefore poorly received. Nor do they exist in the shadow of a brutal past, like the German equivalents of the "five Ds" did. All of those started with the prefix *ent-*, a Nazi favorite, prompting the celebrated chronicler of language Victor Klemperer (1881–1960) to ask whether they are true neologisms or old stock from some surviving fascist word-factory (1966, p. 9).[3] The current chapter's "three Ds" seem comparably unencumbered. Common words, they insist that for the majority, language critique must be an everyday choice, akin to the Cold War-era Czechoslovak dissident Václav Havel's "attempt to live within the truth" (1985, p. 39).

Distrust: Observing

"All philosophy," Ludwig Wittgenstein noted in his much-admired *Tractatus Logico-Philosophicus* (1922), is "Critique of language." But, he hastened to add in parentheses, "not at all in Mauthner's sense" (1999, p. 45). Just above, on the same page, came a sigh:

> [m]an possesses the capacity of constructing languages, in which every sense can be expressed, without having an idea of how and what each word means—just as one speaks without knowing how the single sounds are produced. [...] Language disguises the thought; so that from the external form of the clothes one cannot infer the form of the thought they clothe, because the external form of the clothes is constructed with quite another object than to let the form of the body be recognized.

Whether Wittgenstein was cognizant of it or not, his words happened to be an eloquent summary of Mauthner's main argument. Even the philosopher's most-cited aphorisms ("what can be said at all can be said clearly; and whereof one cannot speak thereof one must be silent") were unacknowledged and perhaps unconscious borrowings from Mauthner (Wittgenstein 1999, p. 27). Mauthner was far from irredeemable.

One role model for Mauthner—alongside two other unlikely bedfellows, philosopher Friedrich Nietzsche and Germany's "Iron Chancellor"

Otto von Bismarck—was Goethe. The world literature theorist and champion inspired many with his distrust, "not to say hatred," toward language. Mauthner rushed to interject, however, that distrust and distance are not tantamount to abandonment. This hatred toward one's bread and butter, he clarified, arises out of deep love (Mauthner 1918, p. 215 and 1901, pp. 129–131).

Mauthner's life, a protracted lesson in love, hatred, and distance, was testimony to that. Höritz/Hořice na Šumavě, his birthplace, lay on the remote forested "coast" of landlocked Bohemia, as Shakespeare's *The Winter's Tale* might have it, in Austria-Hungary. Within view of it, German-dialect-speaking enclaves, the so-called language islands, bobbed up and down in the sea of Czech. Affection between the two ethnic groups had been increasingly on the ebb since the 1860s. A Jew, Mauthner benefitted from neither linguistic camp's trove, having never learned the local German dialect and having abandoned mandatory Czech at age four, retaining little sense for it but deep disdain. Prague, where the family would move to provide a better education for the children and where the majority spoke Czech, had even more linguistic privation in store. The city's gift to its newest resident Mauthner was "paper German" (a phrase for which Mauthner himself gets credit), the dry, lackluster surrogate of imperial bureaucracy, of Kafka, and—as the author openly rued—his own prose (Suchoff 2011, p. 55). What belonged to him? Languages—German, Czech, or Jewish—certainly did not. Goethe's distrust was his only patrimony.

And so, language critique started out as a compulsion. Having begun his note-taking as early as 1873, Mauthner was motivated neither by deep knowledge about the subject matter nor by choice. Uninvited, the ideas took possession of him with a might that he could not resist, he recalled (1918, pp. 205–206). And *Contributions to a Critique of Language* do read as though they were written under a spell. The text resembles a mad wizard's cauldron, into which a new ingredient drops at two- to three-page intervals. On occasion, Mauthner resembles the antiquarians whom he mocks. At times, there's a meek attempt to classify language: colloquial "liverwurst simplicity," he writes, isn't the same as the verbal "art form" practiced by the upper crust or as the "thoughtless babble" that the two milieus occasionally share (1901, p. 47). Other passages deal with tropes and semantics: "never and nowhere have synonyms existed," since living language "knows no doubles" (59). Gender as an arbiter of social privilege makes a tentative appearance, too: "language here mirrors social conditions," and those are, Mauthner sternly admonishes, "unequal education and life experience" (56). So does memory, and a slew of other psychological faculties: "language is the liberation from pain by way of remembrance" (85). The author touches on medical research, from phrenology and physiology to psychosomatic medicine: "all arguments about [the interdependencies between] soul and body are nothing but verbal bickering" claiming to offer solutions but providing little but labels (255). There is even room for an amoeba's worldview, which, bereft of the sensual, somehow seems more immediate, more accurate (351). It is small wonder that Wittgenstein, who wrote short paragraphs and numbered his thoughts, despaired at the sheer convolution of it.

And yet, there was a method to Mauthner's madness. Even the dubious examples tie in with the main thread of the work. People, Mauthner insists, share the "conceited superstition" that their senses are "wondrous instruments" of cognition, and that words are aids (351). In reality, his Nietzschean argument went, everything is contingent and accidental. Most contingent, volatile, vague, and unreliable of all, he wrote over a decade ahead of Ferdinand de Saussure's *Course in General Linguistics*, is language. Learning to distrust it, to overthrow "verbal superstition" was the main goal of language critique, which Mauthner elaborated as "conscientious observation and examination" (3).

"Verbal superstition" or, simply, "word fetish" is our blind faith in the word as iron-clad proof of a referenced reality (148). We treat word as God, Mauthner complained—a mistake for two reasons. The first is our tendency to overuse specific words and to rely on them excessively in forging bonds between people; he singled out "freedom" and "virtue" (1918, p. 218). Thinking that words can "help us see," as Solnit puts it, is a delusion in his view. Definitions are fuzzy, plural, never exactly or even adequately identical for any two people—a haunting remnant of de Tocqueville's democratic America in Mauthner's imperial Austria. The second is that language fails to stay in step with the times, and we do little to help it do so. The nineteenth century, Mauthner noted, had once extolled language as a scientific innovation on par with telegraphy and railroads. While the latter two had evolved by leaps and bounds, the former kept stalling. No, word isn't God, Mauthner erupted. It was nothing more than "salted herring," "preserved old goods" (1901, p. 164).

That which made language unsurpassed art material—its fluidity, its polysemy, its impressionistic blur, its deep layers of history—made it a lousy tool of rational cognition, scientific inquiry, communication of knowledge (129). Language was unequipped for the present and even less, for the future. The linguistic deadweight of hackneyed verbiage held people back. Words too "pregnant with history" and the clutter of inscrutable rules fabricated around them cannot propel progress (1918, p. 216). The thought echoed Karl Marx's frustrations with incessant historical tribute-paying from half a century earlier. The making of history, Marx wrote, can draw succor from tradition-borrowing as little as language learning can thrive on constant retranslation into one's mother tongue (1852).

This was critique's moment and role: to strip the historical layers of language, or, in Marx's words, "to forget" the old burdens (Mauthner 1901, p. 272). Only such a cleanse, Mauthner believed, would transform the limp "salted herring" into "a real form of human action" (11).

Mauthner's exasperated sighs did not vanish into thin air, as the relative obscurity of his name may otherwise suggest. They were more than just symptoms of the mood swings of cultural pessimism throughout Central Europe's well-caffeinated turn-of-the-century metropolises (Arens 1982, p. 145). As noted previously, his *Contributions* hovered over Beckett's work in an auratic, indeterminate sense, and remained a mainstay in his Paris library for decades (Ben-Zvi 1980, pp. 185–186). Joyce, with the cherry-picking bias said to be typical of him, reached for the book to secure the philosophical undergirding for *Finnegan's Wake* (Ben-Zvi 1982, p. 144). Among linguists and philosophers, but also far beyond, Mauthner's outpourings of linguistic skepticism advanced to occupy niches of persistent influence. In German-speaking circles, they even begat an unlikely lyrical current, which goes by the sibilant-spiked nickname *Sprachskepsisdichtung*, or "language-skeptical literature." Even more sonorously, they resonate in the voices of dissidents, drawing the contours of linguistic disobedience into the sharp line of a barricade.

Herta Müller is among those dissidents. Within minutes of the call from the Nobel Prize Committee in 2009, a journalist asked her about Romanian. Müller was born in a tiny Romanian Banat village. For her, the Banat German dialect was native, and High German was second-native. She first learned Romanian as a teenager. Predictably for a bilingual writer and a onetime translator, she mapped her two linguistic personalities for the journalist, summing up: "Language has different eyes." Less formulaically, she added a complication: knowing which pair of eyes was helping her write at any given time was indeterminable.[4]

More notable has been Müller's escape from the role of the designated multilingual, in which hyphenated authors are frequently typecast into scripted discussions of language (in the sense of *langage*). Her sparsely worded Nobel Prize speech may be a stylistic antipode to Mauthner's vituperations, but it is their semantic twin nonetheless. Its story is about how seeking to recalibrate individual speech in the Communist dictatorship of Nicolae Ceaușescu and in the wake of fascism led her to writing. She traded the deathtrap of the spoken word for the life trap of the page, as "writing is a silent act, a labor from the head to the hand. The mouth is skipped over" (Müller 2013, p. 28). Her half-silence was an observation post. From it, she watched herself tumble into a "vicious cycle of words," "always ruthless and restive," always in control of her. Some of these words, like "trauma," "deportation," or "damage," overwhelmed with vagueness and didn't transfer well from real life into literature (Müller 2009, pp. 9, 14). Her observation post at once defied the control mechanisms of a society infamous for its surveillance and decried any and all obsessions with control at a personal level too.

Striking is the recognizable gap between the world and the words: "Objects deceive with their materials, and feelings mislead with their gestures. The sound of the words, along with the truth this sound invents, resides at the interface, where the deceit of the materials and that of the gestures come together. In writing, it is not a matter of trusting, but rather of the honesty of the deceit" (Müller 2009, p. 29). The treachery extended from things to concepts, which "have their own truth, and that comes from how they sound. But they aren't the same as the things themselves, there's never a perfect match" (Boehm 2014). Echoing Mauthner's skepticism, "every object becomes steeped with meaning, but the meanings change with the experience of the viewer." And yet, suspicion of language by no means implies resignation. "For me, distrusting language is self-evident," Müller declares to her translator Philip Boehm, "I seek language because I distrust it. And because I don't know at all how one tells the events. [...] And so, it's something artificial. Language is something artificial." The artifice, in the end, leaves room for user as creator—a language detective, who is, again, so much more than a cop.

What use is Mauthner's legacy now? Several lessons emerge. The first is not to expect salvation from language. The point of critique is not to rely on language as a panacea, but to reclaim human agency. As Müller once told novelist Claire Messud,

> language, itself, doesn't exist. It is only what we can do with it. [...] I have learned not to trust language in a dictatorship because I have learned all the things that a dictator can do with it. And language can help to kill. It can help to save. And you can do anything with language but language in itself is nothing without its relationship to humans. (Cruz 2015)

The second lesson is that preservation alone is not enough. Indeed, continuous correction and adjustment—identifying and filling out the obvious vocabulary gaps or asking difficult questions about some languages' starkly gendered foundations—are essential. It is true that constructed tongues like Esperanto often amaze with the openness to individual speakers' contributions. And yet, the work on any language is never done—though speakers routinely and willingly discount themselves as actual on-the-ground contributors to this work. Third, because language changes, dictionaries—our frequent go-to havens and, increasingly, pillars of ethics—may not always be able to keep up. Language detectives can help keep track of the changes—minute and momentous as they may be. Finally, the same word will not mean the same thing to distinct individuals and communities of practice.

Disinterestedness: Compiling

As Müller hints, the labor begins with the hand that compiles. Whatever the degree of automation, a lot still depends on the hand to transmit, manufacture, or record. To take note, in the most literal sense. Recording, in particular, has long built on data-gathering, on compilation. Etymologically, compiling relates to pillaging, by way of Latin *pilare*, to plunder (McGillen 2015, p. 353). Plunder starts with unsystematic capture of things as they are, rather than as they could be: the pillager grasps, if partially, the objects' present significance but may possess no foresight as to their future utility. Such a non-instrumental, agnostic approach defines disinterestedness (Anderson 2001, p. 92).

In the benign form of plunder that compilation has become, the disinterested hand will collect everything without a definite goal in sight. It is only clear that the collection itself is not the end, and that the goal crystallizes slowly in the subsequent tally. Disinterested compilation, consequently, is by no means a mechanical, mindless endeavor. The familiarity acquired in the acts of plowing through, plucking, and organizing material comes to bear upon it. The prospect is the creation of something new, which fashions disinterested compilation into a kind of "positive critique," which we quite desperately need to rid language of the crisis rhetoric that has grown around it and to question our own self-perpetuated disempowerment vis-à-vis its future (McGillen 2015; Anderson 2001, p. 92).

All this, at first glance, is every lexicographer's job description. This is how dictionaries have long come into existence. But a language detective will not just record words.

There are absences. Those who research internal government communications—the East German secret police (Stasi), for example—will notice they make no reference made to the "person," despite the abundance of exceedingly specific nouns like "agent" or "saboteur" (Bergmann 1999, p. 51). Or pick up on taboos on unequivocal words, such as "to lie," which the Stasi replaced with euphemisms (36). Or overabundant neologisms to suggest planned but still invisible changes afoot (56). These instances were secret, but in present-day societies similar omissions exist out in the light of day. They are the first signs of the drift in values and policies.

There are presences, too: the emotional tones, biases, sentence structures. Recycled clichés. Unprompted resignification of words from positive to negative or from neutral to bias-tinged and conversely. Hyperboles. Bureaucratization. Mechanization and militarization. The rising emotional pitch of vocabularies as much as the voices articulating them. The reduction of phrases to acronyms. The spread of religious expressions with a fanatical streak. Abuses of indirect speech, set off by ironic quotation marks. The uniformity of language across registers, social backgrounds, ages. Or, conversely, the extreme fragmentation of meaning. The self-evidence with which all these changes are consigned to acceptance and disavowal. What falls into these or related rubrics is worth recording, interpreting, and publicizing without delay.

One isn't born with innate will or ability to take up such work. Victor Klemperer, a German-Jewish Romance literature professor who drafted the above roster, give or take, learned this first-hand. In 1935, the Nazis forced him into retirement at age 54 without the right of publication and with a pittance of a pension (Wesley Young 2005, p. 46). The resulting "inner immigration" left him to toil on a history of eighteenth-century French literature, in the hope of avoiding in perpetuity any contact with Nazi print sources. Needless to say, no circumstance was forever for a Jew living in Hitler's Germany. And yet, it took Klemperer a long time to register the first Nazi word as such. Once he did, the verbal flood overtook him. His story, which revived language critique for its present-day use, is a lesson for all language detectives-to-be.

One close friend, as Klemperer narrates in his now-legendary *The Language of the Third Reich*, was a gifted engineer. Brisk professional advancement circa 1933 had tied this young man to Nazi ideology. Once in a while, he would pay Victor and his non-Jewish wife Eva a visit. The shapeshifting Nazi verbiage first entered the apartment with him. The visits being friendly and charming, the married couple looked past an astonishing volume of verbal pollution. *Volksgemeinschaft* (the notorious label for the racialized "people's community") or "Jew hype" (the discounted focus on things Jewish) speckled the fabric of conversation. Victor's World War I service in the Military Censor's Office did little to jolt him into vigilance. But one phrase was too stark to be missed: *Strafexpedition*, or "punitive expedition" (Klemperer 1966, pp. 50–52). This gift—in German, *Gift* translates as "poison"—would be the first entry in Klemperer's "philosophical dictionary," started around 1933. From the diaries peppered with the conspiratorial acronym *LTI* (*Lingua Tertii Imperii*), Latin for the language of the Third Reich—a play on the Nazi obsession with acronyms and, fittingly, a performance of oppositional "counterlanguage"—the notes became a book between July 1945 and December 1946 (Wesley Young 2005, pp. 48–51).

A single word can be enough to sound alarm. It can be a symptom of a briskly metastasizing malignancy. Word by word, in Nazi Germany language seized the reins and reigned (in German, *bemächtigen*, from *die Macht*, power) over everyone and everything, Klemperer imagined (1966, p. 29).

With its 36 thematic chapters, Klemper's account of *LTI*, like its near-coeval, Orwell's *Nineteen Eighty-Four* (1949), paints a gruesome portrait of language, unadorned and unapologetically timely. The portrait's subject matter, however, is problematically omnipotent. "Nazism seeped into the flesh and blood of the masses," Klemperer writes, "by way of individual words, expressions, sentence formulas imposed in millions of repetitions" to be interiorized "mechanically and unconsciously" (23). Klemperer interrogates the Nazi language at every step, yet raises few questions about the might of language as such (Wesley Young 2005, pp. 54–55). Here, the word divides and conquers.

Klemperer's vision teeters on the extreme edge of what the linguists Edward Sapir and Benjamin Lee Whorf would between 1929 and the 1950s explain as "linguistic relativity"—"a range of alternative ways in which language might have significant effects on thought" (Wolff and Holmes 2011, p. 254). But the philologist does more than equate words with thoughts. He espouses linguistic determinism, the view that language "is so strong that it can even overwrite pre-existing perceptual and conceptual capabilities" (254). Nazi idiom wipes the user's slate clean, he suggests, to etch new vocabulary onto it indelibly, dictating realities, homogenizing people from all walks of life, thrusting the glassy-eyed populace into everyday fascist micro-ecstasies, and sustaining its grip long after the actual regime's collapse.

But what totalitarianism is ever so total that individual action does not matter? Tellingly, the book has human agency written all over it. As much as the diary that preceded it, it compiles not so much the vocabularies as the life vignettes enveloping them. The acts in which people adopt Nazi language—Klemperer's emphasis is on ordinary citizens—become visible in microscopic detail. The coy scholar does not simply list the instances of religion suffusing the vernacular: he tells the story of the university teaching assistant Paula von B., a gullible blueblood whose traditional beliefs and instincts inconspicuously morph into her faith in "the Führer" (pp. 117–119). He doesn't just emphasize how Jews, too, succumbed to the unlikely charms of the Nazis' supposed linguistic omnipotence but goes straight to the "passionately interested Germanist" and Goethe-lover Elsa Glauber, who stubbornly refuses to see the contradiction in raising her children as Jews and "fanatical Germans" at once (pp. 208–210).

Klemperer's focus on anecdotal evidence, some historians object, weakens his argument (Wesley Young 2005, p. 52). Not so from the language-critical standpoint. The vignettes, to invoke Herta Müller, affirm that language "is nothing without its relationship to humans." Klemperer may insist Nazi language is a kind of decapitating force, but his linguistic dioramas suggest that a sober compiler would be able, somehow, to keep his or her head on.

What is more, the act of compilation ought to spare no one. Klemperer's compendium tests Germans as much as Jews, plundering words from sterile Nazi party offices and exclusionary Jews' Houses, to one of which Victor and Eva would eventually be confined. In the postwar years, Klemperer's critical habit would abide to sweep aside the propagandistic cloak of East Germany, where he settled down in the hope that Communism might purge Nazism (Watt 2000, p. 454). His comment on the "World Day of Peace" celebration in the newly proclaimed German Democratic Republic (GDR) on October 2, 1949, states dryly that "the worn-out formulae of the functionaries no longer have any effect. Old Goebbels merchandise" (Klemperer 2003, p. 300). Critique, crucially, isn't about blaming the Other. It is always principally self-critique.

By the same token, Nazi language isn't quite so all-powerful if small pockets of private resistance continue to exist. Jews mocked the yellow star as *Pour le Sémite*, punning on the name of the famed medal, *Pour le Mérite*. *Himmlersches Reich* (Himmlery kingdom), named after the brute Heinrich Himmler, was the bitterly sarcastic designation for the SS (Wesley Young 2005, p. 55). In fact, one of the study's deficits is that it pays less attention to these small rebellions than to the Nazi impositions, letting the language of the Third Reich drown out any power that its subversive opponents could seize.

The concluding pages recount Klemperer's lifesaving flight from bombed-out Dresden in February 1945; on the eve of the bombing, the Gestapo had ordered the deportation of the city's last Jews, about 70 of them. His yellow star ripped off, the scholar escaped to rural Bavaria with the refugee convoys. There, Käthchen, a working-class Berliner, crossed his path. She was openly skeptical of the self-professed chronicler. "Do you think you are experiencing something special?" she asks, interjecting that millions have it much worse. But Käthchen's own biography makes a more convincing case than do her objections. She, too, was once imprisoned, "for expressions," that is, for having mocked symbols of the Nazi rule. "For expressions" becomes Klemperer's motto as he sits down to write the book that would recover language from the amorphous mass of abstraction and place it into "the hands that held it"—as ever, the hands of individuals (314).

The postwar era provided no manumission from that lingo, Klemperer would observe, as the book went through multiple re-editions to become part of the GDR's canon. Right and left, his unsuspecting compatriots let Nazi lexicon slip into everyday speech. But it was not all dire. More hands joined in and collaborated to take up his work. From the belated but abundant international attention lavished upon this figure—Martin Brady's English translation of *LTI* would appear only in 2000, and the German diaries remained unpublished until 1995—the diarist may strike us as a lone hero-compiler. He wasn't, and his lesser-known co-combatants were crucial for advancing language critique in both parts of divided Germany, uneven as their labors might have been. Language detectives, as isolated as they may seem, rarely work alone. Nor must they agree on everything, not even on basic principles: contestation propels the activity of critique.

Klemperer's fellow-Romance language scholar Werner Krauss (1900–1976), a leftist resistance fighter, spent his prison years writing a satire of the Nazi regime, *PLN: The Passions of a Halcyon Soul* (1946) (Watt 2000, pp. 424–429). Klemperer, in a bout of professional jealousy, pointed a finger at the "curious" similarity between their works' titles. Miffed though he may have been, in 1948 he read Krauss' article "About the Condition of Our Language," published a year earlier in the short-lived East German journal *Die Wandlung*. Krauss, unlike his comrade-turned-nemesis, argued against blaming the German tongue for its speakers' missteps. Words were neither insidious nor irreversibly disfigured—not even describable by way of sweeping characterizations of any sort. Besides, the pockets of resistance to Nazi language, Krauss argued, were much bigger and numerous than Klemperer had assumed. In particular, Krauss rebuffed any allegations about the wholesale militarization of language. Ordinary soldiers—he drew on his first-hand experience—had never adopted the officer corps' Nazi German, but devised a jargon of their own to circumvent the superiors' lexicon. This moment, of course, came long before the *Wehrmacht* would be deemed complicit in many Nazi crimes.

As a co-editor of *Die Wandlung*, Krauss would have been familiar with the influential series of articles "The Dictionary of the Inhuman," by the vocationally diverse trio of Dolf Sternberger, Gerhard Storz, and W. E. Süskind. Appearing between 1945 and 1948, the essays alphabetized the Nazi language crimes by example, lending the list a user-friendly shape. The point, however, was not to reacquaint the readers with this all-too-familiar material, but to stage a defamiliarizing confrontation. As though in a Greek tragedy, the reader would undergo catharsis and emerge cleansed and vaccinated for the future. Or so the authors hoped.

Foreseeably, that never happened, as Sternberger admitted in 1957. That year the co-authors' compilation, edited and revised, reached West Germany, where all three were living at the time. Preliminary insight into the emerging eastern and western postwar orders had left them with the impression that there had developed since 1945 "no pure and new, no more modest and more lissome, no friendly body of language." Despite the compilers' "hopeful confidence," the weekly *Der Spiegel* wrote in a review, the influence of their "labor of purification" had extended only so far. In fact, their own invocation of purity, a recognizable Nazi obsession, indicated one of the underlying factors prompting the fiasco. "The Dictionary of the Inhuman" was in the end no document of historical estrangement, Sternberger conceded, but indeed "a dictionary of current parlance." Eight new words had to be added to the first West German edition, while only two could be excluded as atrophied. The title of *Der Spiegel*'s review, "Supervised German," indexed more than a smidgeon of sarcasm.

This failure wasn't for lack of trying. Following Germany's capitulation, young poets and writers had returned home "distrustful and sensitive" from the front or from captivity (Watt 2000, p. 430). "There was a war, six years long, we came back home from the war, we found rubble and wrote about it," wrote another Nobel Prize laureate, Heinrich Böll, in his programmatic 1952 defense of his generation's uncompromising realism (2015, p. 18). They couldn't bear the pathos of big words and adopted a lexicon as threadbare as their remaining possessions were. A loose collective of writers was formed, Group 47, convening for readings over some 20 years and nurturing (perhaps too zealously) the literary elite in West Germany. Through their ranks, adherents of a so-called clear-cutting literature came up. They penned verses and stories about life's simplest events, laconic short format-works in the simplest of vocabularies. Particularly emblematic was "Inventory," Günter Eich's 1945 poem listing the returnee's scant belongings. "This is my cap, / this is my overcoat, / here is my shave kit / in its linen pouch," it started, continuing much in the same key (Eich 2009). Adjectives were virtually banned. Things were what they were, not what people perceived them to be. If bombed-out Germany hadn't sprawled over miles upon miles of eerie moonscapes, this writing might have come close to Mauthner's image of a linguistic paradise found.

Their model withstood the test of time, as the Russian-Jewish-American journalist Masha Gessen reminisced recently, with an eye to the early post-Soviet period. Then, the language "for describing things [...] in front of your eyes" became salient yet again (2017a). It was certainly better than formulaic drivel or lies, but still "terrible for conveying the contents of your mind or heart. It was constraining."

In Germany after Hitler, however, the incessant word-rubble-clearing was more than just constraining. This lionized radical break with the "sick language" (Widmer 1966, pp. 2, 26) was too shrill to be credible. In the long run, it prompted doubts about the wishful myths around life in the "zero-hour"—about starting with a clean slate. The desire to make something fresh from the few unblemished scraps of language ran the risk of separating the present from the past (Guntermann 1999, p. 18). Another sort of clean-slate delusion—less deadly than that which Klemperer appears to have seen in Nazi language, but just as strident and equivocal—comes into being. "Everything forgets," mused the critic and essayist George Steiner in 1960, "but not a language. When it had been injected with falsehood, only the most drastic truth can cleanse it. Instead, the postwar history of the German language has been one of dissimulation and deliberate forgetting" (1960, p. 41). Linguistic clear-cutting turned out to be a provisional strategy of subsistence, more than any "most drastic truth."

Germany's ruins offer multiple prompts but no cohesive recipe for present-day language detectives. There is one significant takeaway, however. Waiting for the rubble years, when grammars and vocabularies lie around disintegrated, is waiting too long.

Modernity's conundrum has ever been that knowledge grows "scientific only after the most faithful examination of many catastrophes" (Ripley 2008, p. ix). This is an insight from Samuel Henry Prince, a Canadian priest-turned-sociologist of social change who witnessed and intervened in the consequences of two crushing maritime disasters: the sinking of the Titanic in 1912 and the Halifax Explosion in 1917. Surely, disasters have their uses, for prudent seafaring as well as language. As Soviet dissident Lev Loseff put it, even years of censorship can weave silver linings and become "beneficent" for the so-called "arts of resistance" (Loseff 1984; Scott 1990). "If we get to know our disaster personalities before the disaster," writes Prince's twenty-first-century student Amanda Ripley, "we might have a slightly better chance of surviving" (2008, p. xii). Foresight beats hindsight.

The likes of Klemperer and Krauss knew this. But, hounded, imprisoned, or excluded, neither enjoyed the luxury of immediate intervention. Many of us do today, and this extraordinary historical privilege comes with responsibilities. To question caesuras, since disinterested compiling is about capturing continuity as much as change. To record all transformations, no matter the origin. To bear in mind that language is not anthropomorphic—it doesn't actually forget or remember, despite Steiner's mellifluous formulation, neither does it manipulate and rule without our helping hands. To keep track of who orchestrates the changes, who embraces them, how, and why. To not impugn the words of others without scrutinizing our own—those we use, those we love, those we once used or loved. To not reproduce the language we critique without a good and vigilant reason. To not slip language on as a guise, apply it as a layer of gloss, or look in it for a sense of mastery, so alluring but oh so illusory. Already in the 1980s, the feminist scholar and security analyst Carol Cohn began writing extensively about the "militarization of the mind" by way of listening and learning to speak a "technostrategic language," the sort "that is abstract, sanitized, full of euphemisms; language that is sexy and fun to use; paradigms whose referent is weapons; imagery that domesticates and deflates the forces of mass destruction; imagery that reverses sentient and nonsentient matter, that conflates birth and death" (1987, p. 715). Her point about the experts' tendency to cloak the bitter nuclear-securitarian verities in "lively sexual metaphors" remains, sadly, an evergreen in today's contests over which country's leader has "the bigger button" (Cohn 2018).

In addition to not hiding behind language, we ought to not privilege its ruin over tenacity, as Klemperer did. No single real-life entity has yet been able to usurp *all* words, though it is a beloved dystopian conceit. Understanding how oppositional counterlanguages emerge and work, without romanticizing them, matters no less in the work of language critique than understanding the pathways of institutional semanticide. Finally, we must doubt purity and its frequent manifestation, purism. Practices of excising and trimming, which often exhilarate with their acuity and precision, often conceal subtle effects of erasure.

Distance: Including and Excluding

Distance is virtually synonymous with language critique. Its archetypical formula blends mental detachment, social ostracism, and physical remoteness. There is Mauthner, the perennial nomad uprooted from one periphery to another; and Müller, thrice-excluded by those who could have held her close: as a Banat German in Romania, as a Romanian in Germany, as an all-too-critical voice in the Banat German community. There are Klemperer and his wife, keeping track of absurdly bombastic Nazi turns of phrase in Dresden's ramshackle Jews' Houses. These degrees of distance, extrinsic to language itself, are already evident in their complexity. Another, intrinsic kind of distance deserves separate mention: loanwords.

How to handle foreign borrowings and what belongs in this category have long been questions outstripping the brief of lexicography. Despised by nationalists as impure, lambasted by populists as elitist, purged by editors as bloated and incomprehensible, dismissed by champions of transparent writing (Orwell among them) as superfluous, loanwords quickly become symbolic surrogates for persons. A society's tolerance toward foreign words, one senses, is a yardstick for gauging its tolerance toward humans arriving from afar. Are they housed and accepted? Or are they kept outside, as unassimilable aliens? Are they treated to *special fonts* or pull-out diacritics? Conversely, is plain language a welcome symbol of near-universal accessibility? Or is it a variant of eugenics and nativist supremacism? To entangle this further, are all foreign words created equal? Or are some friends and others foes? If so, which human manipulations assign them these distinct roles, and why? The anthropomorphic acrobatics of verbal migration are important to track because they capture how the tears within (a) language connect to those beyond it.

It was no accident that the sharp-tongued Viennese satirist Karl Kraus (1874–1936), often erroneously held up as the founder of language critique, opens his opus *Die Sprache* (*Language*) with not one but two essays addressed to purists. The word "address" ("die Adresse") itself occupies nearly three pages. Kraus traces how its assimilated German instantiation, logistical in scope (e.g., "postal address"), mutes the social gesture of the French original: *s'adresser*, to turn to or appeal to someone (Kraus 1962, pp. 17–18). The purists, while championing the native turns of phrase (*Anschrift*), Kraus argues, fall prey to egoistic delusion and an attenuating of meaning. They believe that the imported, French connotation will go on toiling behind the scenes dutifully, as though an unremunerated theater prompter. Germanic efficiency, by contrast, would receive the star role, keeping the spotlight on the logistical sense. In the shadows, the moral, lofty, dialogical *s'adresser* would unfailingly soften its edges. An exploitative relationship, indeed.

The repercussions of suppressed or forgotten etymologies and cognate kinships, as recent history shows, can be more serious than at first glance.

In English, the word "monument" is a vivid illustration. Its celebratory connotations, etched onto the seemingly unavoidable link to the adjective "monumental," have been difficult to shed. And yet, the original Latin *monēre* means nothing more than "to remind," no pomp and no eulogy. Nothing stupendous or permanent. Were this etymology widely familiar, "monument" could be open to many definitions, as reminders vary in kind. A more language-critical America would house a memory culture that speaks, feels, and plans quite differently in matters of marking shameful pasts and future commemorations. But etymologies are increasingly neglected as "merely" academic or poetic—too uninnovative for the pared-down public school curricula, while online dictionaries exile them to the depths that most scrolls never reach. Thus, the celebratory undertone of "monument" prevails, and with it many of our memory troubles.

The ghost of purism haunted another German-Jewish thinker with a penchant for language criticism, Theodor W. Adorno. In his two programmatic essays, "On the Use of Foreign Words," from the early 1930s, and "Words from Abroad," from the late 1950s, the philosopher and sociologist shifted his critical gaze from the purists to the properties of the loan words themselves. In both cases, the author, having found his British and American exile between 1934 and 1949 painful and debilitating, was motivated by his formative experiences in Germany—the native country that kept giving him the cold shoulder. To feel foreign at home was the destiny that he shared with all loanwords.

There is no way around the fact that Adorno's gaze at his subject matter, as "Words from Abroad" intimates, is the male gaze. He starts out modestly, and historically, by championing foreign words as "little cells of resistance to the nationalism of World War I" (Adorno 1991a, p. 187). But metaphors derail quickly, collapsing into a Freudian abyss of sexual desire. The want for borrowings, the reader will be stunned to discover, is "like the craving for foreign and if possible exotic girls; what lures us is a kind of exogamy of language, which would like to escape from the sphere of what is always the same, the spell of what one is and knows anyway" (187). From these sexualized *métissage* phantasies, "the affective tension that gives foreign words their fecund and dangerous quality arises" (187).

Perhaps those seductive words struck back in an episode that, some say, may have brought on Adorno's lethal heart attack in 1969. It came after a group of young feminist students mobbed him after a lecture, stripping off their bras to accuse him, an old Marxist, of being but an old reactionary. He never recovered from the sight of their naked breasts at point-blank, but the women may have been onto something. In Adorno's deviant language loyalty, the critic's own depressing blind spots lurk. They make a case not only for critique's mandate to change with the times. As the chapter on care makes clear later in this book, such blind spots suggest that language critique in its traditional guise lends even its dedicated practitioners too few of the tools required to register and dissect language's interactional, non-lexico-grammatical properties. Critique, ultimately, is only one among several crucial regimens of linguistic disobedience.

Eventually, Adorno's essay shakes off the misplaced sexist and racist reverie and turns to the more salient sort of danger that the words unmask—the social sort. "On the Use of Foreign Words," written about 20 years earlier, had already broached the topic. It laid bare a surprising nexus between purism and the typical defense of foreign words. Both, the philosopher alleged, disabled their target by denying it its essential "explosive force" (Adorno 1991b, p. 286). Purists saw loanwords' subversive potential and therefore hurried to silence them. Defenders, in the misdirected spirit of tolerance, fought to prove foreign words similar to the native and thus harmless. The result in either case was similarly incapacitating.

What exactly do foreign words explosively divulge, anyway? They are symptoms of the tensions in society's designs—not only in interpersonal relationships but also in the precarious relation between world and word, today as ever. "The more alienated human beings have become from their things in society, the more strange are the words that will have to represent them" (Adorno 1991b, p. 289). The deeper the rift between the order of things and the human attempts to bend this order to their wishes and desires, Adorno concludes, "the more isolated will foreign words necessarily remain." They stand out as "an expression of alienation itself."

The essay "Words from Abroad" make these earlier ideas more culturally specific. After 1945, Adorno has Germany's Nazi history to explicate too. The chasm that foreign words orchestrate is now less one between the material world and the verbal designs for it and more about Germany's incomplete assimilation into West Europe's Romance civilization. Whereas the French had absorbed the Latin substrate and the British had long accepted much superimposition, in Adorno's land of birth Latinisms were left to "stick out" (Adorno 1991a, p. 187). The country suffered and collapsed from the exacerbated failure of that civilizational union, and language put the trauma on display.

There are other functions that hover within foreign words, more unsuspected aspects of what Adorno calls "explosive material." They unmask what Adorno likes to call "the jargon of authenticity," the deceptively simple words that conceal exclusionary or even politically tainted ideology under native masks (1973, p. xxi). They inoculate against the impositions of transparent language, which, he argues, makes manipulation and degradation easier (Adorno 1991a, p. 191). They bear traces of forsaken humane ideals. Foreign words, in short, are a lifeline to the periods that could have been—as well as to "a better order of things" in the future (Adorno 1991a, p. 192).

Around us, foreign words remain an everyday presence to integrate or exclude. Anthropomorphizing them as if they were sentient subjects would be an analytical mistake, but we can think of them heuristically as mirrors of society's unhealed wounds, of ideological holdovers or revivals, of the wrongs that could not be silenced, of miscommunications between the aging words and the newborn phenomena they purport to describe, yet cannot. We must also ask after those foreign words that we will never integrate—and about the languages that don't easily come to mind as lenders, including American Sign Language, which many very young non-deaf children now learn before learning their second mother tongue, only to forget or neglect it later in life.

Having served, as Adorno points out, both pacifists and Nazis, loanwords (like all words) cannot be inherently good or evil (1991a, p. 191 and Wesley Young 1991, p. 81). These days, some borrowings, like "kompromat," arrive uninvited and accompany detrimental political interference. But "oligarchy," "kleptocracy," or "kakistocracy," to name just a few, prove indispensable in identifying many present-day governments' deeply undemocratic, mercantilist, and nepotistic underbellies, keeping a spotlight on them as long as they exist. It is more useful to think of foreign borrowings not as migrants in need of compassion and shelter but as smoke signals and red flags. What do they show and why? When can language no longer absorb them? And what does this "breaking point" mean (Steiner 1960, pp. 36, 38)?

Acceptance

Considering the range of possible settings for developing a historical sense around language critique—most of them non-Western, indigenous, and/or (once) colonized—choosing to foreground the Austro-German case may appear random, or pedantic. But, far from a gleaming exemplar, Germanophone writing has served as the turbulent testing-ground for the fits and starts of "language critique" and relatedly messy operations, such as "language care" (*Sprachpflege*), where the misfires, overreaches, and insights of these endeavors can be viewed in the grandeur and minuteness of their modern historical scene. The circumstances of these practices' emergence and maintenance make it clear that the German-speaking lands aren't an epitome of success, but an illustration of how neither language nor language critique has ever been—as Joan Didion might have it—a "charm against snakes, something that keeps those who have it locked in some unblighted Eden, out of strange beds, ambivalent conversations, and trouble in general" (1961).

Nonetheless, in the wake of successive human-made twentieth-century disasters, the national and international legacy of these practices is substantial in Germanophone writing and public conversations—arguably, more so, so far, than in the United States.

The famed Austrian literary provocateur Hugo von Hofmannsthal chalked up German-speakers' allegedly acute linguistic awareness to the unusually well-documented history of their tongue (Hofmannsthal 1927). And yet, with the century's tide, that ostensibly enviable historical record would swell up to an inglorious compendium, capturing for posterity how the idiom of Kant and Goethe accessorized, transported, and adapted itself to one -ism after the other: nationalism, colonialism, fascism, communism. How to avoid being "submerged by a reality [one] cannot articulate," as James Baldwin (1979) put it, was the question that loomed too large, around every new corner.

Though not always purposefully interlinked or even aware of each other, language-critical voices in Germany have not just been droning on without results or victories to show for it all. Institutions and civic rituals have been taking shape, transforming the vocational guild of language sleuthing from a solitary into a more communal one. Their range has been considerable. From Klemperer's compilation of Nazi language to the German Academy for Language and Literature, founded only three months after the Federal Republic's founding in May 1949; from the (German) Word of the Year, a tradition invented in 1971 by the long-established German Language Society in Wiesbaden to capture societal change in a nutshell, to "language critique" being the rubric under which present-day media language analyses appear; from citizens volunteering submissions for the "Non-word of the Year" to the Federal Agency for Civic Education issuing reminders that "in a parliamentary democracy, language is not automatically democratic," German-speakers' public language advocacy has entered everyday life in ways still unimaginable for English (Piepenbrink 2010, p. 2). Some high school curricula in Germany have incorporated "linguistic reflections" into language and literature classes. An array of non-academic professionals—lawyers, politicians, theologians, certainly journalists—acknowledge that their preoccupation with semantics is distinctly language-critical (Sitta 2000, pp. 95–96).

True, language critique did not forestall Nazism or authoritarian Communism, and its potency in the face of recent surges of populism remains to be tested. Yet, skepticism not only about the content of verbal messages but also about their form has become a meaningful resource for dissenters, alleviating the kind of linguistic helplessness that has befallen today's Anglosphere. Alas, in Germany, this took decades and a country first hijacked, then ruined, then divided—with two sets of vocabularies developing to reflect this fractured history (Stevenson 2002; Schlosser 2005).

The Anglosphere appears to have gradually tapped into this reserve, albeit without a clear acknowledgment. The "Word of the Year" has been adopted in the United States and the United Kingdom, courtesy of the Merriam-Webster Dictionary, the Oxford English Dictionary, the

Cambridge English Dictionary, and others. Ever since then, *truthiness, credit-crunch, selfie, carbon-neutral, -ism,* and *surreal* have held a mirror up to these two presumptively Anglophone societies amid their cultural drift. And yet, this tradition-trafficking has stopped short of its more serious potentials, which demand more active media participation, curricular modifications, and public awareness. The borrowing has been selective.

In the strongholds of the Anglosphere, then, a fourfold shift is due: from theory to practice, from crisis to routine, from minority to majority, from easy to hard. Elsewhere, and on American territory too, related habits have taken hold in niches. They are worth emulating, to debunk our rash expectation that disobedience must by necessity *reject* the status quo, a norm, or a rule. They urge us to heed several fundamentals, without which critique as a prelude to linguistic disobedience—that broad civic conversation about restoring power to language in a democracy—will fail.

First, we need to *accept language as a bare necessity,* as something ordinary and therefore essential—a shared resource, as we say in the introduction, even if actual idiom differs from place to place. Esperanto's chronicler Esther Schor notes that language is not at its core just "the preserve of the educated" but a way to buy groceries, greet officials, and gossip (Schor 2016, p. 28). Many present-day appeals to treasure language, by contrast, underestimate its hands-on work-a-day presence. They elevate language to the holy grail of communication—near-metaphysical, unreachable and yet, inexplicably, corruptible by some unknowable extrinsic agency that is specifically *not ourselves.*

Second, we should *accept a modicum of isolation.* In North America, being alone sufficiently often played a part that was critical in both senses of this word. The transatlantic slave trade robbed the enslaved of their original tongues, exacerbating their displacement, disorientation, and fragmentation. Only the creation of a new counter-idiom, Black English, mitigated these losses in due course. Reflecting on the extended afterlives of those linguistic privations from his vantage point on the remote French Riviera—the geographical separation focusing his lens—James Baldwin observed:

There was a moment, in time, and in this place, when my brother, or my mother, or my father, or my sister, had to convey to me, for example, the danger in which I was standing from the white man standing just behind me, and to convey this with a speed, and in a language, that the white man could not possibly understand, and that, indeed, he cannot understand, until today. He cannot afford to understand it. This understanding would reveal to him too much about himself, and smash that mirror before which he has been frozen for so long. (Baldwin 1979)

Baldwin's forebears shaped language into an alphabet of warning signs against physical and psychological violence, responding to the white majority's abiding segregation strategies. Even the writer's overabundant commas belonged to this kit. They did not affect connection, as commas ordinarily do, but brought to light the brute force of atomization—his focus—instead.

Third, we should consider *accepting linguistic subjectivity as common good instead of neoliberal currency.* Stinginess about language, as Alison Phipps and her colleagues (2017) describe it—hoarding language and hogging it in proprietary ways—can be a private prerogative, or else a prelude to monetizing the verbal treasure trove in publishing, education, leisure, health, or career development. Language is good, we often hear, because it translates into capital, begetting better jobs, more money, longer lives. But accumulating words without rushing to share them with others is not inescapably tantamount to profiteering. "The surest defense against Evil," the émigré Soviet dissident Joseph Brodsky assured his audience in a college commencement address of 1984, "is extreme individualism, originality of thinking, whimsicality, even—if you will—eccentricity. That is, something that can't be feigned, faked, imitated" (1987, p. 385). Something "that can't be shared […] even by [a] minority" (3, 6). For Brodsky, tongue-twisting idiosyncrasies benefitted not so much the self as such, as they perfected "the art of estrangement" (271). Today's graduates would benefit from hearing about this ethical and aesthetic craft—again and again.

Fourth, we must *accept that nobody is exempt in the long run.* Within the privileged majority, segments can also be affected. There, too, isolation can reap its harvest of language consciousness, and did. A memorable instance is the idolized journalist H. L. Mencken's (1880–1956) magnum opus, *The American Language* (1919). This repository of

Americanisms of all stripes (from the dating slang of the 1920s to the non-English "dialects") sprung up amid the discriminatory campaigns against the German-American author's community. This plump heir to Noah Webster's founding-fatherly struggle to emancipate the country's tongue from its British masters pointed the way towards deeper language consciousness, at least for a moment. World War I was raging, and the United States, in the throes of Germanophobia, was zealously renaming frankfurters into hot dogs and sauerkraut into liberty cabbage. Proverbial language loyalty of the rah-rah-patriotic variety was alive and well. The "National Speech League," formed by the National Council of Teachers of English in 1916 to "improve the quality of our speech," in tandem with Theodore Roosevelt's equations of English fluency with patriotism, ensured that gastro-purism was only the beginning. Returning from the two-years-long reporting stint in Germany—Mencken's domestic column, rather too celebratory of Germany, had become a liability for *The Baltimore Evening Sun*—he witnessed the dangerous ripples of English-only advocacy. Mob violence, incarceration, school closings, and a dramatic drop in ethnic book and news publishing haunted his German-American compatriots (Miller 2011, pp. 41, 62–63). To escape these patriotic excesses, the otherwise indomitable reporter withdrew into himself. *The American Language*, his countercultural take on the nation's deregulated symbol, was the outcome of his "involuntary retirement" at the time (Miller 2011, p. 64).

Retreat

Deliberate, if temporary, deferral of community is a primary commitment of critique. The mantra "only connect" has animated discussions of communications, human and technical, since opening E. M. Forster's *Howard's End*, a novel where as many glitches are resolved as created anew (Schor 2016, p. 9; Hilmes 2011, p. 1). However, "only connect," Forster insinuates, was not a reliable solution at the turn of the century. Neither is it the cure-all in our age of hyperconnectivity.

What is community really worth? To judge by the Genesis story of the Tower of Babel, it is fragile but priceless. A people builds a sky-high structure to make a name for itself, and God, outraged, confuses its language to retaliate for the hubris of engineering and name-claiming. Cocooned in this myth, community has been the ultimate trophy for those who think about language.

Forging new language communities—language communities in particular—has loomed large on the roster of humankind's most hopeful visions. Just as much, recovering them has been a mission marred by racial hierarchies and nationalist aspirations. Collectives might beckon with the promise of inclusivity and diversity, especially under the banner of language rights, enshrined in such legal documents as Article 27 of the United Nations' International Covenant on Civil and Political Rights. "In those States in which ethnic, religious or linguistic minorities exist," it reads, "persons belonging to such minorities shall not be denied the right, in community with the other members of their group, to enjoy their own culture, to profess and practise their own religion, or to use their own language."[5] And yet, history offers some chilling reminders of how the same solidary attraction can turn "disciplining and exclusionary" (Joseph 2002, p. vii).

The rise of mother-tongue idolatry underpinned centuries of European encounters with Others, the history of colonialism overlapping with the seventeenth-century "invention" of monolingualism—the belief that one language "can and should do everything on its own," preferably on its own territory (Gramling 2016, p. 13). In Germany more than elsewhere, myths of salvation and self-liberation "from history, hybridity and social divisions, and the horrors of assimilation" long before Adolf Hitler's rise to power germinated in mother-tongue zealotry (Hutton 1999, p. 8). While race stayed mute, language could—and did—scream in deafening choruses. Linguists had marveled at "the Volk-creating power of language" before racialists did. Their vocabulary still resonates across borders in today's linguistics and jurisprudence (Hutton 1999, pp. 3–12).

Putting off the rush toward community cancels the white noise of institutional echo chambers. It filters out the mindlessly recirculated verbiage of public speech and propaganda. It clears space, creating that "sound-proof room" about which Virginia Woolf wrote in her famous essay, where one's own language—and one's thoughts about why it matters—can fledge until ready to flutter (Woolf 1929). It is a metaphorical hermitage, a place of non-conformity and introspection, where one can "sit at home with the cause," as Ralph Waldo Emerson's 1841 turn of phrase had it (2016, p. 27).

The term "voluntary exile" surfaces in discussions of learning other languages (Lahiri 2016, p. 37). Likewise, in the theory and practice of theater and literature—from Bertolt Brecht's "alienation effect" (*Verfremdungseffekt*) to Viktor Shklovsky's "estrangement" (*ostranenie*)—distancing is a familiar device for amplifying consciousness. For dissenting intellectuals and the ostensibly apolitical artists seeking to escape society's tiresome din, estrangement has long been a way out—and then, eventually, back in. It must now inform the realities of English in the United States and beyond.

Distrust, distance, and disinterest tap into a more rigorous regimen of estrangement than parody and irony. Along with ellipsis, periphrasis, redundancy, and other rhetorical means, the latter two have been the trusty weapons of disobedience in anti-colonial or anti-Soviet arsenals. The games of "coding and decoding," in which they engaged creators and their audiences, helped ordinary citizens manipulate the powerful adversary's goals in their own interests (Loseff 1984, pp. 217, 92).

It would appear that little prevents this pair of tools from being relevant to our age. However, the traffic channels have changed, and so have the audiences. Indeed, the entire global political order has passed away—the Cold War order that, if one believes the journalist and critic Peter Pomerantsev, was shaped by unilateral deployment of keywords and tropes (2018). Scholars of oppositional counterlanguages like Loseff inevitably called on "experienced" or "stylistically sensitive," that is, trained readers (56, 101). A self-selecting, delimited group of experts sought to understand what he described as "the Aesopian language" of censorship circumvention. At present, however, social media and digital platforms make such self-selection impossible.

Irony, to conclude with a cautionary tale, is as easily weaponized by neo-Nazis as it is by anti-fascists. Andrew Anglin, the founder of the ultra-right *Daily Stormer*, has helped himself to the style propagated by famously "snarky" left-leaning outlets, especially the legendary *Gawker*, "to draw in Millennial readers" and deploy irony as cover (O'Brien 2017). The intention was to have "non-ironic Nazism" pass for "ironic Nazism," he openly admitted. Today, irony and sarcasm, we must realize, no longer work in the exclusive interest of linguistic disobedience—and linguistic disobedience itself, to echo our introduction, has devolved into an amphibious beast. These resources are now on everyone's tongue, and the tongue, as Özdamar wrote, will twist in any direction.

Notes

1. Translation by Paul Reiter, in *The Kraus Project: Essays by Karl Kraus*, ed. and trans. Jonathan Franzen (New York: Farrar, Straus and Giroux, 2013), 127.
2. Samuel Beckett, *Dream*, 191, cited in Mark Nixon, *Samuel Beckett's German Diaries 1936–1937*, 10.
3. In English: Victor Klemperer, *Language of the Third Reich. LTI: Lingua Tertii Imperii*, edited by Martin Brady. (London: Bloomsbury, 2013).
4. Griehsel, "Interview with Herta Müller."
5. International Covenant on Civil and Political Rights," December 16, 1966, http://www.ohchr.org/EN/ProfessionalInterest/Pages/CCPR.aspx, accessed on September 19, 2017. See also, Moria Paz, "The Failed Promise of Language Rights: A Critique of the International Language Rights Regime," *Harvard International Law Journal* 54:1 (Winter 2013): 159–160.

References

Adorno, Theodor W. "On the Use of Foreign Words." Vol. 2 of *Notes to Literature*, edited by Rolf Tiedemann and translated by Shierry Weber Nicholsen, 285–291. New York: Columbia University Press, 1991a.

Adorno, Theodor W. "Words from Abroad." Vol. 1 of *Notes to Literature*, edited by Rolf Tiedemann and translated by Shierry Weber Nicholsen, 185–199. New York: Columbia University Press, 1991b.

Adorno, Theodor W. *The Jargon of Authenticity*. Translated by Kurt Tarnowski. Evanston: Northwestern University Press, 1973.

Anderson, Amanda. *The Powers of Distance: Cosmopolitanism and the Cultivation of Detachment*. Princeton: Princeton University Press, 2001.

Arens, Katherine M. "Linguistic Skepticism: Towards a Productive Definition." *Monatshefte* 74, no. 2 (1982): 145–155.

Baldwin, James. "If Black English Isn't a Language, Tell Me, What Is?" *The New York Times*, July 29, 1979. http://www.nytimes.com/books/98/03/29/specials/baldwin-english.html.

Beech, Hannah. "'No Such Thing as Rohingya': Myanmar Erases a History." *The New York Times*, December 2, 2017. https://www.nytimes.com/2017/12/02/world/asia/myanmar-rohingya-denial-history.html?smid=tw-nytimesworld&smtyp=cur&_r=0.

Ben-Zvi, Linda. "Fritz Mauthner for *Company*." *Journal of Beckett Studies* 9 (1984): 65–88.

Ben-Zvi, Linda. "Mauthner's *Critique of Language*: A Forgotten Book at the *Wake*." *Comparative Literature Studies* 19, no. 2 (Summer 1982): 143–163.

Ben-Zvi, Linda. "Samuel Beckett, Fritz Mauthner and the Limits of Language." *PMLA* 95, no. 2 (March 1980): 183–200.

Bergmann, Christian. *Die Sprache der Stasi. Ein Beitrag zur Sprachkritik*. Göttingen: Vandenhoeck & Ruprecht, 1999.

Blankenhorn, David. "Blue Said, Red Said." *The American Interest*, March 7, 2018. https://www.the-american-interest.com/2018/03/07/blue-said-red-said/.

Boehm, Philip. "Herta Müller: The Art of Fiction No. 225." *The Paris Review* 210 (Fall 2014). https://www.theparisreview.org/interviews/6328/herta-muller-the-art-of-fiction-no-225-herta-muller.

Böll, Henrich. "Bekenntnis zur Trümmerliteratur." *Der literarische Zaunkönig* 3 (2015): 18–20.

Bourdieu, Pierre. *Language and Symbolic Power*. Translated by Gino Raymond and Matthew Adamson. Cambridge: Polity Press, 1991.

Brodsky, Joseph. *Less Than One. Selected Essays of Joseph Brodsky*. New York: Farrar Straus Giroux, 1987.

Cohn, Carol. "Sex and Death in the Rational World of Defense Intellectuals." *Sign* 12, no. 4 (1987): 687–718.

Cohn, Carol. "The Perils of Mixing Masculinity and Missiles." *The New York Times*, January 5, 2018. https://www.nytimes.com/2018/01/05/opinion/security-masculinity-nuclear-weapons.html.

Confessore, Nicholas et al. "The Follower Factory." *The New York Times*, January 27, 2018. https://www.nytimes.com/interactive/2018/01/27/technology/social-media-bots.html.

Cruz, Cynthia. "Notes toward a New Language: On Herta Müller." *The Poetry Foundation Blog*, April 13, 2015. https://www.poetryfoundation.org/harriet/2015/04/notes-toward-a-new-language-on-herta-muller-.

Dent, Susie. *Dent's Modern Tribes: The Secret Languages of Britain*. London: John Murray, 2016.

Dickson, Andrew. "Inside the OED: Can the World's Biggest Dictionary Survive the Internet?" *The Guardian*, February 23, 2018. https://www.theguardian.com/news/2018/feb/23/oxford-english-dictionary-can-worlds-biggest-dictionary-survive-internet.

Didion, Joan. "On Self-Respect: Joan Didion's 1961 Essay from the Pages of Vogue." *Vogue*, October 22, 2014 [1961]. https://www.vogue.com/article/joan-didion-self-respect-essay-1961.

Dyussu, Nanda. "An Interview with Ngũgĩ wa Thiong'o." *The Los Angeles Review of Books*, April 23, 2017. https://lareviewofbooks.org/article/an-interview-with-ngugi-wa-thiongo/.

Eich, Günter. "Inventory." Translated by Joshua Mehigan. *Poetry* (April 2009). https://www.poetryfoundation.org/poetrymagazine/poems/52394/inventory-56d230d30ccb8.

Emerson, Ralph Waldo. *Self-Reliance and Other Essays*. Middletown, DE: CreateSpace, 2016.

European Commission. *A Multi-Dimensional Approach to Disinformation*. Luxemburg: Publications Office of the European Union, 2018. https://ec.europa.eu/digital-single-market/en/news/final-report-high-level-expert-group-fake-news-and-online-disinformation.

Felski, Rita. "Critique and the Hermeneutics of Suspicion." *Journal of Media and Culture* 15, no. 1 (2015). http://journal.media-culture.org.au/index.php/mcjournal/article/viewArticle/431.

Foucault, Michel. "What Is Critique?" In *The Political*, edited by David Ingram, 191–211. Oxford: Blackwell, 2002.

Gardner, Anthony. "All Curators Now." *1843 Magazine*, November/December 2013. https://www.1843magazine.com/content/ideas/anthony-gardner/all-curators-now.

Gauger, Hans Martin. *Über Sprache und Stil*. Munich: C. H. Beck, 1995.

Gessen, Masha. "The Autocrat's Language." *New York Review of Books*, May 13, 2017a. http://www.nybooks.com/daily/2017/05/13/the-autocrats-language/.

Gessen, Masha. "What Words Mean." *Topic* 5 (November 2017b). https://www.topic.com/masha-gessen-what-words-mean.

Gilbert, Glenn G. "Review of *Sprachnorm, Sprachpflege, Sprachkritik: Jahrbuch des Instituts für Deutsche Sprache 1966/67*, edited by Hugo Moser, Hans Eggers, Johannes Erben and Hans Neumann." *Language* 47, no. 4 (December 1971): 984–990.

Goethe, Johann Wolfgang von. "Maximen und Reflexionen 1033." Vol. 12 of *Goethes Werke. Hamburger Ausgabe in 14 Bänden*, edited by Erich Trunz, 511. Munich: C. H. Beck, 1978.

Grady, Constance. "The Complicated, Inadequate Language of Sexual Violence." *Vox.com*, November 30, 2017. https://www.vox.com/culture/2017/11/30/16644394/language-sexual-violence.

Gramling, David. *The Invention of Monolingualism*. New York and London: Bloomsbury Academic, 2016.

Guntermann, Georg. "Einige Stereotype zur Gruppe 47." In *Bestandsaufnahme: Studien zur Gruppe 47*, edited by Stephan Braese, 11–34. Berlin: Erich Schmidt Verlag, 1999.

Havel, Václav. *The Power of the Powerless: Citizens against the State in Central-Eastern Europe*, edited by John Keane and translated by Paul Wilson. Armonk, NY: M. E. Sharpe, 1985.

Hilmes, Michelle. *Only Connect: A Cultural History of Broadcasting in the United States*. Boston: Wadsworth, 2011.

Hofmannsthal, Hugo von. *Wert und Ehre Deutscher Sprache* [1927]. http://gutenberg.spiegel.de/buch/wert-und-ehre-deutscher-sprache-6190/1.

Hutton, Christopher M. *Linguistics and the Third Reich: Mother-Tongue Fascism, Race and the Science of Language*. London: Routledge, 1999.

Joseph, Miranda. *Against the Romance of Community*. Minneapolis: University of Minnesota Press, 2002.

Kant, Immanuel. *Critique of Pure Reason. Unified Edition*. Translated by Werner S. Pluhar. Indianapolis, IN: Hackett Publishing Company, Inc., 1996.

Kaplan, Alice. *Dreaming in French: The Paris Years of Jacqueline Bouvier Kennedy, Susan Sontag, and Angela Davis*. Chicago: The University of Chicago Press, 2012.

Karatsareas, Petros. "A Deadline to Speak English Would Betray Britain's Long History of Multilingualism." *Quartz*, March 23, 2018. https://qz.com/1235544/a-deadline-to-speak-english-would-betray-britains-long-history-of-multilingualism/.

Kelly, John. "Everything is Weaponized Now. This is a Good Sign for Peace." *Slate*, August 30, 2016. http://www.slate.com/blogs/lexicon_valley/2016/08/30/how_weaponize_became_a_political_cultural_and_internet_term_du_jour.html.

Klemperer, Victor. *Die Unbewältigte Sprache—Aus dem Notizbuch eines Philologen—"LTI."* Darmstadt: Joseph Metzler Verlag, 1966.

Klemperer, Victor. *The Lesser Evil: The Diaries of Victor Klemperer, 1945–1959.* Translated by Martin Chalmers. London: Phoenix, 2003.

Kraus, Karl. *Die Sprache.* Munich: Kösel-Verlag, 1962.

Lakoff, George. "Don't Retweet Donald Trump and Don't Use His Language." *Deutsche Welle English*, January 21, 2018. http://www.dw.com/en/dont-retweet-donald-trump-and-dont-use-his-language/a-42213110.

Lahiri, Jhumpa. *In Other Words.* Translated by Ann Goldstein. New York: Alfred A. Knopf, 2016.

Latour, Bruno. "An Attempt at a Compositionist Manifesto." *New Literary History* 41 (2010): 471–490.

Loseff, Lev. *On the Beneficence of Censorship: Aesopian Language in Modern Russian Literature.* Munich: Otto Sagner, 1984.

Macfarlane, Robert. *Landmarks.* London: Penguin Books, 2015.

Marx, Karl. *The Eighteenth Brumaire of Louis Bonaparte* [1852]. https://www.marxists.org/archive/marx/works/1852/18th-brumaire/.

Mauthner, Fritz. Vol. 1 of *Beiträge zu einer Kritik der Sprache.* Stuttgart: J. G. Cotta'sche Buchhandlung Nachfolger, 1901.

Mauthner, Fritz. *Erinnerungen.* Munich: G. Müller, 1918.

McGillen, Petra. "Kompilieren." In *Historisches Wörterbuch des Mediengebrauchs*, edited by Heiko Christians, Matthias Bickenbach, and Nikolaus Wegmann, 352–368. Cologne: Böhlau, 2015.

Miller, Joshua L. *Accented America: The Cultural Politics of Multilingual Modernism.* New York: Oxford University Press, 2011.

Monbiot, George. "Forget 'the Environment': We Need New Words to Convey Life's Wonders." *The Guardian*, August 9, 2017. https://www.theguardian.com/commentisfree/2017/aug/09/forget-the-environment-new-words-lifes-wonders-language.

Moyd, Michelle and Yuliya Komska. "Donald Trump Is Changing Our Language. We Need a Vocabulary of Resistance." *The Guardian*, January 17, 2017. https://www.theguardian.com/commentisfree/2017/jan/17/resist-donald-trump-vocabulary-resistance-rhetoric.

Müller, Herta. "Nobel Lecture: Every Word Knows Something of a Vicious Circle." In *Herta Müller: Politics and Aesthetics*, edited by Bettina Brandt and Valentina Glajar, 20–30. Translated by Philip Boehm. Lincoln: University of Nebraska Press, 2013.

Müller, Herta. *Ich glaube nicht an Sprache: Herta Müller im Gespräch mit Renata Schmidtkunz.* Klagenfurt: Wieser, 2009.

O'Brien, Luke. "The Making of an American Nazi." *The Atlantic,* December 2017. https://www.theatlantic.com/magazine/archive/2017/12/the-making-of-an-american-nazi/544119/.

Orwell, George. "Politics and the English Language." Vol. 4 of *The Collected Essays, Journalism and Letters of George Orwell,* edited by Sonja Orwell and Ian Angus, 127–140. New York: Harcourt Brace Jovanovich, 1968.

Özdamar, Emine Sevgi. "Mother Tongue." In *Mother Tongue,* 9–15. Translated by Craig Thomas. Toronto: Coach House Press, 1994.

Piepenbrink, Johannes. "Editorial." *Aus Politik und Zeitgeschichte* 2 (2010): 2.

Pomerantsev, Peter. "Jokes and the Death of Narratives." *The American Interest,* March 24, 2018. https://www.the-american-interest.com/2018/03/24/jokes-death-narratives/.

Rafael, Vicente. *Motherless Tongues: The Insurgency of Language amid Wars of Translation.* Durham: Duke University Press, 2016.

Remnik, David. "Putin's Four Dirty Words." *The New Yorker,* May 5, 2014. https://www.newyorker.com/news/news-desk/putins-four-dirty-words/amp.

Reston, Laura. "The NRA's New Scare Tactics." *The New Republic,* October 3, 2017. https://newrepublic.com/article/145001/nra-new-scare-tactic-gun-lobby-remaking-itself-arm-alt-right.

Ripley, Amanda. *The Unthinkable: Who Survives When the Disaster Strikes.* New York: Crown Publishers, 2008.

Rogers, Daniel. "The Uses and Abuses of Neoliberalism." *Dissent* (Winter 2018). https://www.dissentmagazine.org/article/uses-and-abuses-neoliberalism-debate.

Schlosser, Horst Dieter. *Es wird zwei Deutschlands geben. Zeitgeschichte und Sprache in Nachkriegsdeutschland, 1945–1949.* Frankfurt: Peter Lang, 2005.

Schor, Esther. *Bridge of Words: Esperanto and the Dream of a Universal Language.* New York: Metropolitan Books, 2016.

Scott, James C. *Domination and the Arts of Resistance: Hidden Transcripts.* New Haven: Yale University Press, 1990.

Si, Jeannette. "The Chinese Language as a Weapon: How China's Netizens Fight Censorship." *Medium,* June 21, 2017. https://medium.com/berkman-klein-center/the-chinese-language-as-a-weapon-how-chinas-netizens-fight-censorship-8389516ed1a6.

Silverman, Jacob. "In Our Cynical Age, Nobody Fails Anymore—Everybody 'Pivots'." *The New York Times Magazine*, August 29, 2017. https://www.nytimes.com/2017/08/29/magazine/in-our-cynical-age-no-one-fails-anymore-everybody-pivots.html.

Sitta, Horst. "Was publizistische Kritik sein könnte." In *Reflexionen über Sprache aus literatur- und sprachwissenschaftlicher Sicht*, edited by Axel Gellhaus and Horst Sitta, 95–114. Tübingen: Max Niemeyer Verlag, 2000.

Snyder, Timothy. *On Tyranny: Twenty lessons from the Twentieth Century*. New York: Tim Duggan Books, 2017.

Solnit, Rebecca. "The Case of the Missing Perpetrator: On Mysterious Pregnancies, the Passive Voice, and Disappearing Men." *Literary Hub*, February 11, 2016. http://lithub.com/rebecca-solnit-the-case-of-the-missing-perpetrator/.

Solnit, Rebecca. *The Mother of All Questions*. Chicago: Haymarket Books, 2017.

Steiner, George. "The Hollow Miracle. Notes on the German Language." *The Reporter*, February 18, 1960. 36–41.

Stevenson, Patrick. *Language and German Disunity. A Sociolinguistic History of East and West in Germany, 1945–2000*. Oxford: Oxford University Press, 2002.

Suchoff, David. *Kafka's Jewish Languages: The Hidden Openness of Tradition*. Philadelphia: The University of Pennsylvania Press, 2011.

Thompson, Mark. *Enough Said: What's Gone Wrong with the Language of Politics?* New York: St. Martin's Press, 2016.

Van Hulle, Dirk. "Nichtsundnichtsundnichts: Beckett's and Joyce's Transtextual Undoings." In *Beckett, Joyce, and the Art of the Negative*, edited by Colleen Jaurretche, 49–62. Amsterdam: Rodopi, 2005.

Watt, Roderick H. "*Landserprache, Heeressprache, Nazisprache?* Victor Klemperer and Werner Krauss on the Linguistic Legacy of the Third Reich." *The Modern Language Review* 95, no. 2 (April 2000): 424–436.

Weil, Simone. "The Power of Words." In *Selected Essays, 1934–1943: Historical, Political, and Moral Writings*. Translated by Richard Rees. Eugene, OR: Wipf & Stock, 1962.

Wesley Young, John. "From LTI to LQI: Victor Klemperer on Totalitarian Language." *German Studies Review* 28, no. 1 (February 2005): 45–64.

Wesley Young, John. *Totalitarian Language: Orwell's Newspeak and Its Nazi and Communist Antecedents.* Charlottesville, VA: University Press of Virginia, 1991.

Widmer, Urs. *1945 oder die "neue Sprache." Studien zur Prosa der "jungen Generation."* Düsseldorf: Pädagogischer Verlag Schwann, 1966.

Wittgenstein, Ludwig. *Tractatus Logico-Philosophicus.* Translated by C. K. Ogden. Mineola, NY: Dover Publications, 1999.

Wolff, Philip and Kevin J. Holmes. "Linguistic Relativity." *WIREs Cognitive Science* 2 (May/June 2011): 253–265.

Woolf, Virginia. "A Room of One's Own" [1929]. http://gutenberg.net.au/ebooks02/0200791h.html.

3

Correction

Correction and the Mother Tongue

In 1986, the prolific Gĩkũyũ novelist, playwright, essayist, and memoirist Ngũgĩ wa Thiong'o published *Decolonising the Mind: The Politics of Language in African Literature*. The volume pulled together four essays Ngũgĩ had written and presented to audiences across Africa and Europe in the first half of the 1980s. By the time *Decolonising the Mind* came out, Ngũgĩ had published four English-language novels, as well as short story collections, plays, and more. But in *Decolonising the Mind*, Ngũgĩ announced to his readers a change of course—a correction—in his writing life. Following his 1977 novel *Petals of Blood*, Ngũgĩ had "said farewell to the English language as a vehicle of [his] writing of plays, novels, and short stories," with all of his "subsequent creative writing [being] written directly in Gĩkũyũ language" (1986, p. xiv). He had continued writing "explanatory prose" in English. But *Decolonising the Mind*, Ngũgĩ announced at the beginning of the book, was his definitive "farewell to English as a vehicle for any of [his] writing. From now on it is Gĩkũyũ and Kiswahili all the way." He hoped "to continue dialogue with all" through translation (Ngũgĩ 1986, p. xiv). And he has in fact done so,

© The Author(s) 2019
Y. Komska et al., *Linguistic Disobedience*,
https://doi.org/10.1007/978-3-319-92010-8_3

continuing to publish at an astonishing clip, engaging in trenchant, sometimes visionary critique, and always aspirational in imagining a better world.

Ngũgĩ's correction grew out of his profound disappointment and anger that African writers found themselves living in ostensibly independent, postcolonial nation-states, but still wrote mainly in the languages of the colonizers—English, French, and Portuguese. Confounded by what he saw as a serious stumbling block to African peoples' liberation, he pointed to language as foundational: "[w]riters who should have been mapping paths out of [...] linguistic encirclement of their continent also came to be defined and to define themselves in terms of the languages of imperialist imposition. Even from their radical and pro-African position, in their sentiments and articulation of problems they still took it as axiomatic that the renaissance of African cultures lay in the languages of Europe" (5). The corrective Ngũgĩ offered in *Decolonising the Mind* ran as follows: African writers should write in their first languages because they "carr[ied] the content of our people's anti-imperialist struggles to liberate their productive forces from foreign control." In postcolonial settings, first languages such as Gĩkũyũ did not carry the same nationalist aspirations that had once fashioned their European counterparts into instruments of domination. Nor were they privileged linchpins of monolingualism, "linked to an exclusive, clearly demarcated ethnicity, culture, and nation," as in western settings (Yıldız 2012, p. 2). Rather, they were presumed, at the outset, to be at home in societies where multilingualism is the norm (29).

Ngũgĩ also believed that African peoples needed to care for and cultivate their languages in order to meet "the challenge of creating a literature in them, which process later opens the languages for philosophy, science, technology and all the other areas of human creative endeavours" (29). Using the language of "African Renaissance," Ngũgĩ's call for writing in African languages was conceived as a necessary step for African peoples as they undertook the difficult work of making nations out of former colonies. In this effort, he found company with other African intellectuals such as Julius Nyerere, the president of neighboring Tanzania, who worked tirelessly to cultivate and elevate the East African lingua franca Kiswahili as Tanzania's national language. He aimed to make Kiswahili a point of pride for the new nation's citizens, even as Tanzanians also continued to speak indigenous languages—117 of them—in their homes, communities, and regions, and in different spheres of their lives (Simons and Fennig 2018).

Calling for solidarity with the "organised peasantry and working class" people, Ngũgĩ recognized that to "open out African languages" for them to use in liberatory politics might invite charges of subversion, even treason, by "neo-colonial" state leaders (30). Ngũgĩ knew what he was talking about. He had been detained in a Kenyan jail from 1977 to 1978 for his play *I Will Marry When I Want*, which criticized the government. He went into exile after his release from prison. He believed these were risks worth taking: "The call for the rediscovery and the resumption of our language is a call for a regenerative reconnection with the millions of revolutionary tongues in Africa and the world over demanding liberation" (108). For Ngũgĩ, writing in one's first language was a necessary corrective for grounding future liberatory work. In a sense, however, designations "first," "second," and so forth mattered less in the "receptively multilingual" (ten Thije and Zeevawert 2007) environment of Kenya, a country of nearly 70 languages, where speakers of different tongues often have no trouble understanding each other. Something more universal was at stake. African and other peoples could draw on linguistic and cultural wellsprings the colonizers had cast as inferior, and in consciously choosing to use their first languages for a full range of expression, could reclaim them for anti-colonial and anti-capitalist work. Indeed, to him, "the real language of humankind" was "the language of struggle." Liberation could not come through continued use of the colonizing languages. Cultivation of first languages as dynamic languages that could accommodate literature, science, technology, and all other realms of human achievement, was fundamental to meaningful political change. And in fact, political change would be incomplete without linguistic change: by making heard the voices of people who spoke languages other than those of the colonizers, new political expression would filter into wider discourse, enabling new political possibilities.

Ngũgĩ's departure from the conventions of literary production among African writers in the 1970s and 1980s as expressed in *Decolonising the Mind* reminds us that language is the beating heart of political and social activism. Although writing as a citizen of postcolonial independent Kenya, his critique, and the correction he undertook to address it, also speaks to this chapter's subject. Ngũgĩ's effort to decolonize his mind by writing in Gĩkũyũ initiated a life-long quest for modes of truth-telling expression against neocolonial efforts to stifle such truths. Along the way, he generously championed collaborative work taking place between "Black scholars on either side of the Atlantic." In his Foreword to the pathbreaking 2002 edited volume *Black Linguistics*, he wrote that it was "one more step on the road toward the decolonization of Black languages and Black thought" (Makoni et al. 2002, p. xii). He was not the first to choose to write and publish in African languages. But *Decolonising the Mind* marked a turning point, because it made explicit the link between the politics of language and decolonization well before it became a staple of postcolonial theory (Ngugi 2018).

Linguistic disobedience in the age of Trump also requires a form of decolonization of the mind: rebuilding civic language means proclaiming that language matters, and proving that point in as many interactions as possible. If our language has been colonized by empty neoliberal concepts and business-speak, then the correction must be to assert the language of struggle—the "revolutionary tongues"—as counterweights, indeed, counterlanguages. In addition, correction can help fill out the dangerous vapidness of such language, providing alternatives that affirm human potential, dynamism, and liberatory ideals. The language of struggle must become our mother tongue. Increasing numbers of ordinary people are awakening to what activists have long known—that doing politics requires vigilance, effort, and focused attention. These same people can also take courage from knowing that the languages they already have are up to the task, if they decide to use them.

What Is (a) Correction?

The Merriam-Webster dictionary has become a subversively critical voice since November 2016 in part by tweeting out corrections that simultaneously troll the Trump administration. "The sassiest dictionary on Twitter" intervened in the relentless stream of falsehoods emanating from the 45th

President's mouth by insisting that words have meanings, and that those meanings make a difference in everyday parlance and politics (Lee 2017). For example, after Donald Trump included the word "unpresidented" in one of his now infamous and predictable early-morning Twitter rants in December 2016, Merriam-Webster tweeted a definition of the word "HUH" ("—used to express surprise, disbelief, or confusion, or as an inquiry inviting affirmative reply"), preceded by the following comment: "Good morning! The #WordOfTheDay is … not 'unpresidented'. We don't enter that word. That's a new one." Or, in January 2017, when Trump's advisor Kellyanne Conway argued that the President's falsehoods were instead "alternative facts," Merriam-Webster reminded its followers that "a fact is a piece of information presented as having objective reality."

Merriam-Webster's tweets buoyed the spirits of its already Trump-weary followers, putting on a clinic for defending the power of language, and asserting its place in shaping political publics amidst the Trump administration's single-minded focus on undoing anything that had an Obama signature on it. Some of Merriam-Webster's Twitter appeal—its followers number in the hundreds of thousands—certainly comes from the expert trolling its tweets dish out on a regular basis. Perhaps it also appeals because of its careful focus on *correcting* word usage, pulling a concerned public back to the centrality of everyday language practice as a bulwark against all that Orwell warned us of in the 1940s. Of course, dictionaries must also be treated with caution, since their tendency to fix language in place makes them susceptible to falling out of date. They can also be exclusionary, since words must meet a certain threshold of usage before they become entries. They can purvey norms and enforce standards, many of which we question in this book. Still, there is great appeal in the image of a nerdy dictionary site doing battle with a political leadership that tramples on language in more ways than anyone dared imagine a mere few years ago. It provides a "vision of sanity" in an age of manipulation, uncertainty, and lies (Tannen 1981, p. 145). It gives those interested in thinking together about words' meanings, their shifts, their fluidity, a common place to start, an anchor in a storm. And the dictionary's digital presence makes it more responsive to the pressing need for correction than would have been possible in the age of the big book.

What, then, is (a) correction? According to Merriam-Webster, our favorite subversive dictionary, correction is "the action or an instance of correcting, such as (a) amendment, rectification (b) rebuke, punishment (c) a bringing into conformity with a standard (d) neutralization, counteraction." It lists an additional three possible definitions as well, including "a decline in market price or business activity following and counteracting a rise," and of course the one that reminds us that we have an entire tier of government devoted to "corrections"—the one that incarcerates millions "as a matter of public policy." But for now, let us focus on "the action or instance of correcting" in the age of Trump.

Like critique, correction is essential to linguistic disobedience, a practice that urges a constant probing for better ways to express ideas with accuracy, differentiation, sensitivity. Alongside critique and care, it should be foundational to everyday linguistic practice. It should cause one to be aware of context, to practice vigilance in how one uses language and to what ends, and to courageously intervene in conversations in order to jolt others into reckoning with their own speech and its consequences. Consider for example a widely circulated clip from MSNBC's *Live with Stephanie Ruhle* that aired in August 2017. Ruhle and her co-host, Ali Velshi, refused to allow presidential advisor Brad Thomas to lie about Trump's supposed positive impact on the stock market and jobs creation: "You can't just lie on T.V. I don't know who your people told you you were coming on T.V. with, but you cannot lie about the economy to us," said Velshi (Jones 2017). In this and the rest of the exchange, Ruhle and Velshi corrected Thomas several more times, refusing to cede space to his characterizations of Trump's economic impact.

In doing so, they accomplished two things. First, they fully occupied their status as veteran financial analysts and journalists. As Velshi put it to Thomas live on air, "You should fire your press person because if they didn't tell you that you were coming on T.V. with Velshi and Ruhle, who I think collectively—I don't want to give away Stephanie's age—but between the two of us we have been doing this for about 50 years. This is a silly conversation to have with us." Notwithstanding the dangers of experts participating in exclusionary language practices of their own, viewers of Ruhle and Velshi's show could nonetheless take heart in their ability to use evidence to counter a Trump appointee whose presence on the show seemed to merely take up space. Second, they interrupted Thomas's attempt to push a narrative thin on evidence and thick with the dissembling that had become so recognizable by the time this show aired. They became heroes for a news cycle simply by refusing to allow a government official to lie without challenge. There have of course been many such instances in journalism—Anderson Cooper's meme-worthy eye-roll while talking to Kellyanne Conway, or sportscaster Jemele Hill's tweet labeling the President a "white supremacist" come to mind as viral examples of journalists going into the breach with Trump and his surrogates.

Journalists elsewhere have also taken on this labor. During a press conference at Trump's March 2017 Berlin meeting with Chancellor Angela Merkel, German journalist Kristina Dunz asked him directly about the hypocrisy of his continual decrials of "fake news" while he also perpetuated a stream of unfounded allegations about Barack Obama's supposed wiretapping of Trump's offices (Faiola and Kirchner 2017). Her question, and additional ones posed by a German colleague, modeled how to challenge Trumpspeak. And outside of the United States' political and media landscape, the journalist Liang Xiangyi's disgusted eye-roll at a fellow journalist's softball question during China's annual National People's Congress meeting in March 2018 went viral on Chinese social media until government censors intervened (Mozur 2018). Journalistic disruptions such as these offer glimpses of different ways to correct authority figures and the media cultures that cater to them. Witnessing and discussing these corrections in real-time or via social media have become mainstays for those reeling from the stream of untruths that invade each news cycle. These corrections, many of them non-verbal, serve as reminders that critical thought still thrives among many media professionals. Their everyday challenges to Trumpspeak open tiny pockets of breathing room in what often feels like a sinking ship.

Perhaps first and foremost then, *correction is interruption*. Interruption redirects thoughts for reconsideration, and encourages hesitation before acting. Reconsideration is an opportunity for growth. Hesitation is an opportunity to choose a different action. Parents learning how to manage their toddlers' tantrums learn to interrupt undesirable behaviors—by changing the child's scenery, using a silly voice, or giving them an exciting new activity to keep them occupied. In a way, and without simplistically comparing adults to errant children, correction is also about interrupting language to encourage reflection on what has just been said, and instilling a prompt to think before using that formulation again. In writing, parentheses often interrupt. When a reader sees parentheses, she must stop to consider what's between them and why. Recasting slightly Hannah Arendt's suggestion in *The Human Condition* that we practice "thinking what we are doing," in an echo of critique, we can think of correction as opening up possibilities for urging others to "think what they are saying" (1958, p. 5).

Interruption also lets those within earshot know that something is being disrupted. A change in tone and accompanying gestures signal to those listening that there has been a shift. Perhaps it causes some to tune in more closely, while others tune out. The point is not that the interruption will immediately change how people think, but that the moment of disruption itself may be generative in unpredictable ways. This applies to what we do not want to hear as well. As important as it is to defy disruptive language that speaks with the goal of harming others—think of Trump's casting of Mexican immigrants as rapists, or his characterization of Muslims as terrorists—tuning out entirely is a dangerous tack. In this case, the interruption is a siren alerting us to stay vigilant, to challenge, to begin caring not only about our own language but also the language of others. If Trump is the Disruptor-in-Chief, our civic duty is to hear and correct, not because we think it will change him, but because it might change us, sharpening our abilities to critique, tuning our senses to the dangers of callousness and apathy. We hear and correct not in order to achieve interactional advantage, but to do better in our own language practices, bit by bit.

There are no guarantees, of course. One correction does not preclude the need for additional interventions, and occasions sometimes arise sooner than we'd like. Each time a correction is offered, it is an opportunity to consider the content of the words we choose and use, how they cause harm or buoy hopes, how they change conversational dynamics and micro-political discourse. Correction should prompt us to make better choices, to own when we don't quite measure up, and to commit to doing better. Correction might require confrontation and urgency, or it might require patience. Either way, letting people slide without correction squanders opportunities to shift the terms of debate, to educate, to address a wrong, to chip away at interactional hegemony and its projections of authority.

During a talk at the National Women's Studies Association Conference in 1981, Audre Lorde reeled off a list of "examples of interchanges between women" that were infused with racism. Here is one: "I wheel my two-year-old daughter in a shopping cart through a supermarket in Eastchester in 1967, and a little white girl riding past in her mother's cart calls out excitedly, 'Oh look, Mommy, a baby maid!' And your mother shushes you, but she does not correct you. And so fifteen years later, at a conference on racism, you can still find the story humorous. But I hear your laughter is full of terror and dis-ease" (Lorde 2007, p. 126). From other remarks in the talk, it is clear that Lorde is addressing an audience of white women, to whom she is speaking her truth, offering her correction. Their laughter, "full of terror and dis-ease," gives her audience an opportunity to accept or deflect. Either way, Lorde's practice of linguistic disobedience held up a mirror to white feminism, demanding that those in the sisterhood make their own corrections in their everyday lives. Lorde, an exceptional poet who knew the workings of language inside and out, made the purposeful choice to break the rules: where she should have used "unease," she instead used her poetic sensibility to indict white feminism for its racism. "Dis-ease" evoked racism as sickness.

Not everything can or should be corrected on the spot. We must always pick our battles, making sure to read the context we are entering, knowing the risks we may be undertaking. When and where can a student in a classroom correct their teacher? When does a woman in a board room point out that a man has taken something she just said, repackaged it, and presented it as his own without acknowledging her input? When does a person with a disability call out someone for using able-ist words and concepts, or supporting able-ist practices? When and where can a faculty member with less authority than a campus administrator correct their language choices? As a practice of linguistic disobedience, correction continues to operate within all the socio-cultural and socio-economic hierarchies that discipline our behaviors. The point is to recognize that and forge ahead so that the challenge being issued has a chance to take hold in the minds of those listening. And a qualifier: there is surely much more to learn here from those who specialize in teaching and learning, especially those who have developed criticisms of classroom hierarchies and the utility of correction in those environments. Let us try.

Approaching conversations with a listening mindset that hears what needs correcting, and then sensibly addresses it, in the appropriate tone, pitched at the right level, is the first step toward this style of linguistic disobedience. As a practice of linguistic disobedience, the goal should be to remind people—gently, forcefully, with humor, with vulnerability, or angrily should the case warrant it—that they do not know everything, and perhaps more importantly, that they can learn from a correction. Not all will tolerate such confrontations well. (And let us be honest. These are, in fact, mini-confrontations. They are not easy, or at least, they are not easy for everyone.) After all, correction can feel like a personal attack, dredging up feelings of inadequacy, which often lead to angry responses or refusal to engage. Rejection is a potential outcome that should be anticipated, heard, and accepted. But it should not prevent continued efforts to make corrections. The vitality of our political language depends upon it. In the words of essayist Kiese Laymon, "we owe it to our teachers and our children to imagine new routes into beauty, health, compassion, citizenry, and American imagination. We owe it to each other to love and insist on *meaningful revision* until the day we die" (Laymon 2013, p. 21). Or to use Audre Lorde's formulation, expressing anger at racism rather than keeping it quiet can be a "corrective surgery" that allows growth. On the other hand, "guilt and defensiveness are bricks in a wall against which we all flounder; they serve none of our futures" (Lorde 2007, p. 124).

Who Can Make Corrections?

Making corrections should not be the province solely of experts. In fact, if we think about how people become experts, we notice that they became so via a process that almost certainly involved being corrected repeatedly. Experts may in fact know a great deal about their chosen area, but they also frequently know and acknowledge how much they don't know. When I was in graduate school, I wrote a paper surveying the historiography of women and war. As a novice in the field, I ended up making an arrogant, dismissive, and ultimately wrong claim about the state of African women's history. My dissertation advisor, a pioneering scholar of gender and ethnicity in pre-colonial African history, corrected me based on her expertise. By pointing out to me all that I had missed in my attempt to capture the state of the field, and by giving me a mediocre grade to reinforce my need for improvement, she made a deep impression on me. I rarely assume anymore that topics have yet to be written on, and try to avoid making such sweeping claims. As painful as her correction was, it was vital to my ability to progress as a scholar. It was also a bracing lesson in acknowledging the many feminist scholars who had painstakingly worked to narrate histories of women in Africa when there *really* wasn't much to build on. My advisor's correction shifted how I think about the field, but it also shifted my relationship to my profession, demonstrating for me how collegiality and generosity work to propel us forward to new inquiry. To the extent that I now think of myself as an expert on African soldiers in the German East African colonial army, for example, it has come from a process of constant correction.

But expertise in any formal sense is not a requirement for correcting others. Experience, too, is a powerful basis for challenging the assertions of those who have not had certain experiences. Fundamentally, such challenges invite people to reckon with difference, to contemplate incorporating other lives into their political thinking, and to question their assumptions. Here, another personal example. Early in 2017, I was the last person to leave a conference room in our student union at the end of a meeting. A member of the building's custodial staff—a white woman—came into the room to prepare it for the next meeting. We exchanged pleasantries, and then she continued: "Boy, Trump sure is cleaning house, isn't he?" I froze. With Trump's administration in the midst of issuing a blizzard of executive orders, I was not sure where this statement was going, and I didn't really want to know. But she continued, revealing her dismay over policies she believed would hurt people like her. She expressed frustration that more people in her community either had not voted, or had not thought through the implications of Trump's election for their lives. Her description of Trump's actions as "cleaning house" was a source of anguish for her, not a victory lap. Relieved, I conversed with her as a fellow traveler. In this exchange, she corrected me, even if she didn't know it. Assuming from her initial remark that we would have little in common, I imagined that she was about to cross over into territory I did not want to traverse. I was wrong. By speaking her experience, and by disrupting my assumptions about her, I learned something about my own limitations, my own tendencies to disengage, my own stereotyping practices. I was interrupted, and I now stand corrected. Politeness kept me in the room. My decision to hear her out allowed me to change my mind, to correct my thoughts, to give up some of my urge to have the interactional advantage.

To answer the question that frames this section then, anyone can make corrections, and anyone can be corrected. People correct each other every day. A mispronounced name. A miscalculated bill. A poorly chosen word in a sentence. Any of these might move a person to ask for a correction, and under these kinds of circumstances, people typically oblige, fixing the error, perhaps offering an apology in the process. These form the basis of many mundane interactions. The power of an apology lies in acknowledging that one has made an error. It is a self-correction that restores fairness to an interaction—however small—gone wrong. In theory, there is no reason that this process can't also occur in settings where there is an imbalance of power or authority. If a colleague, a boss, or an authority figure uses outmoded, offensive language or codes to refer to an individual or a group, she should be corrected. A public figure who mischaracterizes history for political purposes should also be corrected. States that flout their founding documents should be constantly reminded of their hypocrisy, as Czechoslovakian human rights activists like Václav Černý and Václav Havel did in 1977 with Charter 77, a document comprised "in its entirety of quotations of passages from the State Constitution" (Černý 1985, p. 125), which illustrated all the ways the state was failing to live up its supposed ideals. A "language warrior" or language detective invested in linguistic disobedience will make a correction, prioritizing accuracy and the opportunity to reframe things, even at substantial risk. At a minimum, these risks might include causing discomfort among friends, co-workers, family members, and others. At worst, these risks might include arrest, loss of livelihood, imprisonment, injury, or death. It is important not to minimize the harm that might come to those who correct authority figures. At the same time, it is important to remind each other that censoring ourselves, or failing to offer correction when it is needed, or obeying our impulses to be polite or to reassure others by not challenging them—these responses only reproduce stasis, and stasis does not put us on a moral path toward just and fair social and political relations.

Risking Correction

Those who have assumed such risks in the interest of correcting political and social discourse embody the spirit of linguistic disobedience. We could choose from many examples: Sojourner Truth and Ida B. Wells, Rosa Luxemburg and Emma Goldman, Martin Luther King, Jr., and Malcolm X, Rigoberta Menchú and María Julia Hernández. The details of their labor as language warriors and language detectives, however, often get lost in the smoothed out stories we tell about them as heroes, martyrs, and revolutionaries. But in reading their writings, speeches, and other forms of communication, we see the building blocks they used in their own practices of linguistic disobedience. Steve Biko, a student leader and anti-apartheid activist who helped found the Black Consciousness Movement in South Africa, is a case in point. In the 1970s, Steve Biko articulated the frustrations and aspirations of millions of young South Africans living under the brutalities and depredations of apartheid. With Nelson Mandela and other members of the African National Congress imprisoned or living in exile, Steve Biko was part of a generation of young anti-apartheid activists who faced down the state, often enough paying with their blood for their truth-telling. As a leader of the South African Students' Organisation (SASO), and later the Black Consciousness Movement, Biko voiced unwavering opposition to apartheid. He also emerged as an uncompromising advocate for black liberation. In 1971, he spoke to fellow SASO members about the meanings of blackness and the essence of Black Consciousness. He pointed out that the organization's policy manifesto "defined blacks as those who are by law or tradition politically, economically and socially discriminated against as a group in the South African society and identifying themselves as a unit in the struggle towards the realisation of their aspirations" (Biko 1986, p. 48).

He went further, arguing that "merely by describing yourself as black you have started on a road towards emancipation, you have committed yourself to fight against all forces that seek to use your blackness as a stamp that marks you out as a subservient being" (48). Biko insisted that black people work to correct their thinking, moving away from destructive thoughts that would allow them to "willingly surrender their souls to the white man," and toward those that would instead allow them to "hold their heads high in defiance" of the apartheid state (49). He advocated for "black solidarity," by which he meant solidarity among the different categories of people experiencing oppression under white minority rule—Africans, Coloureds, and Indians—who had often "[held] each other in contempt" rather than working together to defeat their common enemy—the apartheid state (52). The work of Black Consciousness was the work of "correcting false images" of black people in South African educational and religious institutions, of becoming "[their] own authorities rather than wait[ing] to be interpreted by others" (52).

Biko's intellect sparkled through his writings and the documents that recorded the words he spoke in various settings in his all too short life. Subjected to numerous arrests and detentions because of his political work, Biko was nevertheless relentless in correcting white South African assumptions about blackness, embodying in the process the central tenets of Black Consciousness. Consider this exchange, taken from evidence Biko gave in a 1976 trial. The trial involved state charges against SASO and the Black People's Convention (BPC)—both organizations that Biko was involved with—over their participation in a banned rally celebrating the recognition of a Frente de Libertação de Moçambique (FRELIMO) government in neighboring Mozambique.[1] The defense lawyer, Advocate David Soggot, pressed Biko to explain the point of "conscientizing" black people. In Soggot's mind, the permanence of apartheid's socio-economic hardships and violence obviated the need for anti-apartheid activism:

Soggot: The question I want to put to you is this, haven't these people [i.e., black people living in townships] got used to and come to accept their, what you call, existential conditions, their grievances, insecurity, the absence of food or inadequate food and so on?

Biko: That is I think understating the position. I think it is possible
          to adapt to a given hard situation precisely because you have
          got to live it, and you have got to live with it every day. But
          adapting does not mean that you forget; you go to the mill
          every day, it is always unacceptable to you, it has always been
          unacceptable to you, and it remains so for life, but you adapt
          in the sense that you cannot continue to live in a state of con-
          flict with yourself. [...] You cannot keep answering back to
          him [i.e. a higher-ranking white employee] every day: don't call
          me boy, don't shout at me, don't swear at me, because there is
          also the element of the job that he has got to keep. He had
          adapted but he does not forget it, and he does not accept it,
          which I think is important. (Biko 1986, pp. 114–115)

Biko corrects and disrupts Soggot's formulation of the permanence
and naturalization of apartheid and black people's roles therein. Soggot
asks for a confirmation of black apathy in the face of oppression, but Biko
refuses. Instead, he renders a black person full of complexity, dignity, and
strength despite living with apartheid's evils. Biko criticizes the degrada-
tions of South African "influx control" policies using a structural argument, eschewing the notion that better "application" of methods would
improve black people's experiences of mobility (111). At each turn, Biko
counters the state's attempts to paint apartheid as benign with clear evidence of its malignancy. In so doing, his linguistic disobedience rein-
forces the "righteousness" of Black Consciousness as a corrective to
apartheid's fantasies about controlling blackness. And each time he spoke
for black people's emancipation and the mental work it required while
living in a racist society, he offered his fellow black South Africans the
correctives they needed to at least distance their identities from the apartheid state's unceasing efforts to destroy them, providing them a means of
self-preservation under oppressive conditions.[2]

Biko incurred terrible risk each time he undertook such corrective
work, and yet, he never stopped doing it. In 1973, he was "banned" by
the apartheid state, which placed severe restrictions on his ability to
assemble with others, to speak in public, and to travel. He was arrested
and detained many times. Finally, in August 1977 he was arrested and

detained for the last time. He died in custody in September, his body horribly abused, revealing the awful evidence of tortures experienced at the hands of South African police. His fight against apartheid had come to an end. It is easy to imagine that his linguistic disobedience continued through his final detention. Several months before he was taken into custody for the last time, he remarked to an interviewer on the power of surmounting "the personal fear of death":

> [I]n interrogation the same sort of thing applies. I was talking to this policeman, and I told him, "if you want us to make any progress, the best thing is for us to talk. Don't try any form of rough stuff, because it just won't work." [...] If they talk to me, well I'm bound to be affected by them as human beings. But the moment they adopt the rough stuff, they are imprinting on my mind that they are police. And I only understand one form of dealing with police, and that's to be as unhelpful as possible. So I button up. And I told them this: "It's up to you." (Biko 1986, p. 152)

Linguistic disobedience comes in many forms, including the decision to be silent in the face of state violence. In the United States, the right to remain silent shapes legal processes designed to protect individuals from incriminating themselves. To "read someone their rights" is to acknowledge this right to silence. But beyond the legal realm, the decision to remain silent in the face of overwhelming state power can also be a form of linguistic disobedience. Biko's correction to the policeman interrogating him was to remind him, with words, that they were both human. If they were not going to use words anymore, then he would continue fighting in silence, without them.

"Your silence will not protect you," Audre Lorde wrote that very same year in a paper delivered at the Modern Language Association's annual academic conference (Lorde 2007, p. 41). Her words are all the more striking when considered alongside Biko's purposeful invocation of silence in the interrogation room when threatened with physical violence. Lorde summoned women and other marginalized people to find "the words they [did] not yet have," arguing that fear should not be honored "more than [their] own needs for language and definition" (41, 44). Breaking the silence was her foremost political objective. Reconciling these two positions on silence—Biko's and Lorde's—requires recognizing silence as part of the communicative field. It is not an empty void, but rather, can be empowering or disempowering depending on the context where it is being used. Critique, as the second chapter of this book argues, emerges from silence, from the quiet that permits detachment and observation. For Biko, silence was a corrective to the unequal power in the interrogation room, his response to the policeman's insistence on interactional hegemony predicated on violence. Lorde rejected silence because it was a symptom of the unequal power inherent in being a queer black woman.[3] In both cases, silence was generative, and thus a vital part of linguistic disobedience.

Welcoming Correction

And what happens when someone corrects me? Or you? Ideally, I hear it and turn it over in my mind. Perhaps I am jolted into rethinking my position. I accept the correction, learning from it and incorporating the new knowledge into my future thoughts and actions. Or I dig in, refusing to consider the possibility that I might be wrong. Or perhaps I pause to consider that I might be wrong, but reject the correction anyway. Or I argue, attempting to convince the person who has corrected me that they might not be right. Perhaps I avoid or deflect it because the correction insults me, or worse, it threatens the core of my being, and I can't find the words, evidence, or method to argue. Being on the receiving end of a correction can be generative, stultifying, or inconsequential. But starting from a stance of linguistic disobedience makes it possible to welcome the chance to consider what the correction means and what to do with it.

Reverend William J. Barber II, a leader of the Poor People's Campaign, and prior to that a founder of the Moral Mondays movement in North Carolina, learned the value of correction while helping his parishioners in Martinsville, North Carolina, start a union. As he began actively supporting his parishioners' unionization efforts, he quickly encountered the limits of thinking of them as a monolith, learning "they were not of one mind" (Barber 2016, p. 17). Some supported the union because they saw civil rights and workers' rights as inextricably linked. Others rejected unionization out of worry that companies would not operate in places where unions made demands on them, thereby depriving the community of jobs. "Listening to the analysis of both sides," he recalled, "my mind had to acknowledge the legitimate concerns and at least partial truth of each party" (17). He remained committed to forming a union "because it was the right thing to do," but in the end, the effort failed. This formative experience trained Barber to "struggle intellectually toward a new imagination of faithful social engagement" (39). Propelling him were a series of corrections that came from multiple directions: his parishioners, his readings across theological, historical, and political science scholarship, and his recognition that race and class intersected in local politics in ways that cried out for new social justice formations.

What he learned from this moment he later applied to the building of a "moral movement" that draws on a combination of civil disobedience, coalition-building, and different forms of engagement to ensure dynamism (127–130).[4] In the Poor People's Campaign, he and other clergy have organized to bring together "tens of thousands of people across the country to challenge the evils of systemic racism, poverty, the war economy, ecological devastation and the nation's distorted morality."

The many corrections and concessions that it takes to build a movement and the inherent shift from focus on the individual to the collective, as explained by Reverend Barber, reveal instances of linguistic disobedience. Take for example the first of the Poor People's Campaign's "Fundamental Principles": "We are rooted in a moral analysis based on our deepest religious and constitutional values that demand justice for all. Moral revival is necessary to save the heart and soul of our democracy."[5] The Campaign's commitment to "moral analysis" and "moral revival" invites questions about what constitutes morality, for whom, and under what circumstances. The authors of the Campaign's Fundamental Principles have clearly anticipated such potential challenges, but they do not adopt a defensive posture. Take, for example, Principle 7:

> We aim to shift the *distorted* moral narrative often promoted by religious extremists in the nation from personal issues like prayer in school, abortion, sexuality, gun rights, property rights to systemic injustices like how our society treats the poor, those on the margins, the least of these, women,

children, workers, immigrants and the sick; equality and representation under the law; and the desire for peace, love and harmony within and among nations [emphasis ours].

This well-crafted principle uses the word "distorted" to reclaim the domain "morality" from "religious extremists" who have tried to claim it in the service of *their* politics. The Campaign's principles prioritize the *systemic* over the *personal* in an effort to overturn the many injustices faced by "the least of these"—the marginalized parts of society enumerated in the principle. And it extrapolates to a wider world, referencing "peace, love and harmony within and among nations." In this and the other Fundamental Principles of the Poor People's Campaign, linguistic disobedience manifests in the refusal to traffic in violent imagery, political brinksmanship, or social exclusion. Infused with the language of struggle, it promises a return to a campaign of "sustained nonviolent civil disobedience [...] as a way to break through the tweets and shift the moral narrative." Civil disobedience and linguistic disobedience go hand in hand, even though their theoretical discussions and formulations, as we lay out in the introduction, have yet to catch up to this realization.

What Is (Was?) Political Correctness, and What Is It Not?

It would be remiss for a chapter about correction not to address the topic of political correctness. To do so is also to wade into a now decades-long tussle between left and right over words, what they contain, and why they are worth fighting over, or correcting. In this little book, by training our focus on how correction as interruption works with and against "political correctness," we want to shift away from knee-jerk responses to bad words, and toward two kinds of work. First, the work of disruption, and second, that of identifying troublesome words and exploring what they contain in order to problematize their usage.

Political correctness has long been perceived on the right as a silencing mechanism or a bludgeon wielded by the left—as a kind of "language police." They complain that people on the left are too sensitive, too wedded to "identity politics," too eggheaded. "Lighten up, they're just words," they say. Or, "can't you take a joke?" More perversely, they either juxtapose political correctness with what they deem *real* dangers in the world, or they equate political correctness with actions that might destroy the United States. As Laila Lalami outlined in an April 2016 essay in *The Nation*, "To hear some people tell it, there is no greater threat to the Republic at the moment than political correctness. It forces dissenters to cower before views they would ordinarily reject, out of fear that they will be labeled as bigots. It thwarts attempts at finding common-sense solutions to the country's problems" (Lalami 2016). Donald Trump, Ted Cruz, John Kasich, and many others have made political sport of casting "political correctness" as a monstrous obstacle to their patriotic efforts to save the country from supposed dangers posed by immigrants, radical Muslims, transgender people in search of bathrooms they can use, and college students seeking safety from bullies or sexual assault (Itkowitz 2015). Increasingly, a retooled sensibility around political correctness is being used to foster community on the right. They even cynically deploy it now for their own purposes. White supremacist Richard Spencer, for example, evokes the idea of the "safe space" to argue that white people are under threat, and therefore in need of a white ethno-state—a safe space— where peoples of European descent can live without the bother of living with other, darker, populations (Mendoza 2017).

This conservative and right-wing co-opting of concepts that had been liberal staples has in fact created an opportunity. It has revealed hypocrisies, blind spots, and euphemisms within liberal politics that merit deep consideration. In June 2015 Hillary Clinton gave a speech at Christ the King United Church of Christ, a historically black church in Florissant, Missouri, one week after the massacre of nine African-Americans in another historically black church in Charleston, South Carolina. The Florissant church is not far from Ferguson, where mass protests followed the killing of the unarmed African-American teenager Michael Brown by a cop in August 2014. In her speech, she used the phrase "all lives matter" while making a point about the importance of acts of kindness in helping people overcome difficult times (Keith and Kelly 2015). Her message was a sound one. But her use of "all lives matter" struck a dissonant and to many, offensive, chord: why did she use this phrase in a black church, among people reeling from the state's deadly violence against Michael Brown and more broadly against communities like theirs? In a time when so many white Americans refused to acknowledge that Black lives matter, why did Clinton assert that all lives matter?

In the spirit of correction as interruption, a language warrior will ask these questions without fear in order to call attention to what is contained in that phrase—all lives matter—and to ask people to examine why it might be used. By now, the patterns are quite clear. The use of "all lives matter" touts an assumed equality and democracy that does not yet exist. While the sentiment is alluring, it is false. Saying that "black lives matter," on the other hand, embraces the evidence that shows time and again that people of color in the United States and elsewhere bear the brunt of inequality, injustice, and state violence. Based on that evidence, those who assert that black lives matter implicitly also point out the lie in the phrase "all lives matter." The critique of "all lives matter" is not political correctness. It is in fact a radical act. It is linguistic disobedience.

But won't this kind of criticism simply enable the right and other unsympathetic actors to continue bashing such work? Why criticize liberal language choices when there are worse problems out there? The work of correction outlined here is intended to better prepare those of us who claim to care about justice and equality to undertake the political work necessary for moving in that direction. Linguistic disobedience is a different way of thinking about the work that has always been done by people who are thoughtful about language. They do not engage in this work because they want to be "politically correct." They do so because they recognize that language has tremendous power and authority in shaping how we think and talk about people, places, and history; that words have meanings rooted in history, which is dynamic, not static; and that when people claim language for themselves, they are actively shaping their identities in conversation with the communities they value.

To value these things and to fight for them must invariably involve correction. What is perceived by some as mere political correctness is usually simply a demand for heightened attentiveness to words' meanings, how usage creates meanings, and how sloppy usage generates equally sloppy ideas. When it comes to correction, many on the left and right sides of the political spectrum balk at being pushed too far in the direction of unsettling their unquestioned privilege, however it manifests. But this can be an *opportunity* for those who see themselves as striving for liberation, and who see critique and care of language as fundamental work in achieving those things in everyday language practice. There is a practical equivalent in the soul-searching that many journalists have undertaken in the past year. Here, David M. Shribman at the *New York Times* reflects: "The president's taunts have prompted long-overdue if uncomfortable and unwelcome reflection in our newsroom and others. But it has also prompted all of us to be more humble, more careful and more dedicated than ever to the basic elements of our craft: to marshal facts, produce stories and pay little mind to criticism, whether from left or right. To show, by our work, that the truth still matters" (Shribman 2017). The rejection of criticism Shribman expresses here is perhaps worrisome, but it is hard to argue with his central point, that truth-telling matters.

Let us take an example from education. Those who teach African history have long had to engage in the work described above as a foundational classroom practice (alongside the venerable tradition of the map quiz!). Students often come to African history courses with deeply ingrained assumptions about African peoples and their history. Most of these ideas come from the way that the continent's peoples are represented in various media, including popular films depicting Africans as impoverished or violent, news reportage that covers catastrophes and violence but ignores or sidelines other kinds of stories, and book covers that depict the continent as a place of lone baobab or acacia trees in the midst of otherwise uninhabited space (Keim and Somerville 2018, pp. 13–32). Animals talk, but people don't. Think about the last time you read or heard something about Africans or the African continent. Chances are that it fit one of these tropes. As Kenyan author Binyavanga Wainaina's widely circulated piece "How to Write about Africa" sarcastically admonishes: "In your text, treat Africa as if it were one country. It is hot and dusty with rolling grasslands and huge herds of animals and tall, thin people who are starving. Or it is hot and steamy with very short people who eat primates. Don't get bogged down with precise descriptions" (Wainaina 2006). We read this and laugh at Wainaina's scathing satirical critique. Yet it also hits close to home. People really *do* write this way about Africa, and they can be strangely allergic to correction.

In teaching students about Africa then, professors nudge their students to make better choices in how they represent the continent and its peoples. This work starts with gentle correction, asking students to own and acknowledge the images, stereotypes, and tropes that have formed for them a kind of knowledge base about Africa. But this knowledge base is in fact largely devoid of content about African peoples, their lives, cultures, histories, economies, relationships, politics. Rather, they are filled to overflowing with simplistic racist caricatures. Worse, these caricatures and the words used to evoke them are so commonplace that students sometimes resist unlearning them. And yes, they sometimes think that their professors are imposing political correctness on them, making them choose one word over another without good reason.

But we have every reason in the world to insist on these corrections. Take for example the ubiquitous use of the word "tribe" as a shorthand for talking about African polities and societies. Like a reflex, when people begin talking about Africa, the word "tribe" comes tumbling out. Why is this a problem? Because the word "tribe" stands in for a plethora of inaccurate and ahistorical things that are going unsaid. As Keim and Somerville put it, "*tribe* is frequently American code for primitive" (Keim and Somerville 2018, p. 115). The word contains decades of racist characterization of Africans as backwards, savage, uncivilized, violent, hopeless. Its use becomes a destructive shorthand, replacing thought. It permits lazy thinking, while proudly trafficking in base, simplistic representations of Africans. It relieves people from doing the work of accepting African peoples as fellow human beings.

The alternative to this simplistic way of thinking and talking about Africa is to ask students to do the work of *naming* Africans as they would want to be named, to talk about their politics *as* politics, to resist the urge to simplify a vast and complicated place that is over three times the size of the continental United States. We ask them to resist generalization and dehumanization in the interest of learning how to think about Africa as a dynamic place with a history, a place shaped by mobility and ingenuity, a place of learning and erudition and technological innovation. The point is not to deny that Africa has many dire problems that make people's lives difficult in myriad ways. Instead, the point is to correct the assumption that Africa is *only* the sum of its problems. The point is to hold up to students all of the historical processes and structural inequalities that have contributed to the making of African poverty, environmental disaster, and conflicts, asking them to confront and question their simplistic assumptions.

Students quickly grasp that using the word "tribe" (and there are others as well, such as "savage," "native," "hut," or "witch-doctor" that make the list) is not the right answer (Aizenman 2017). This is the easy part. Some become genuinely interested in and accustomed to making better choices about how to talk, write, and think about Africans. They sit with the discomfort of not quite knowing how to refer to peoples, histories, and politics that are unfamiliar. Still, there are always a few who resent this correction, feeling that it is an example of liberal "political correctness," that such focus makes mountains out of molehills (it's just a word!), an undue focus on a word which, after all, some Africans even use to describe themselves. They resist.

To counter this tendency, professors explain to students that the history of "tribes" in Africa emerged not from a deep past, not from a ahistorical time, but out of the very concrete histories of twentieth-century colonialism. European colonizers sought out ways of categorizing the array of peoples they encountered in the territories they claimed to control. Once these categories were established, they made it possible for colonial officials to label them "tribes" for their own administrative purposes. African peoples participated in these categories to differing degrees, but usually not as a manifestation of some sort of timeless belonging to a "tribe." Rather, they negotiated their political identities to minimize the harm of not doing so or to benefit in certain ways. In the profoundly unequal political hierarchies that defined colonialism, which laid the basis for independent nation-states, the notion of tribe largely ignored African self-understandings, affinities, networks, communities, and political arrangements in favor of simplified, fixed, timeless categories that insisted on drawing lines between groups. Teaching African history in the United States thus must always start by establishing what kind of language works and what does not in seeking to understand Africa and Africans beyond the rampant stereotypes that deny them full humanity in everyday discursive and representational practices. It must start from a place of linguistic disobedience, where correction of unexamined assumptions and injurious language undergirds the educative process, with the hope that students' thought patterns about Africa will be interrupted, redirected, and applied to fuller understandings of Africans as participants across the entire range of human experience. And this teaching should not be limited to the classroom. Journalists, politicians, readers, workers, movie-goers all could use vaccination against stereotyping Africa and booster shots on how to improve how they think about and engage the continent in their everyday lives.

Fighting with conservatives and others over what words mean and why they matter is perhaps a waste of time. "Tribalism," a fraught word that now appears in writing about US politics with increasing regularity, seems to foreclose opportunities for meaningful engagement across party lines (Fallows 2017). But fighting for words' meanings, contesting the use of words that have been emptied of useful meaning, and choosing words that best convey a striving for justice and equality are not mere political correctness. These corrections are as vital as any other. Caving in to accusations of political correctness in the interest of political expediency or in order to avoid confrontation cedes valuable spaces of interruption to those who either do not care about language, or who want to take it in directions that will thwart the goals of linguistic disobedience.

Reducing this concern for language to "political correctness" does a disservice to those who are fighting every day for the words they want to use to describe themselves, their communities, their politics, and their visions of justice. Patrisse Khan-Cullors, a founder of Black Lives Matter has been labeled a "terrorist" for her activism against the deadly policing of black people. In her memoir, Khan-Cullors rejects this label, placing it instead where it belongs: "And if ever someone calls my child a terrorist, if they call any of the children in my life terrorists, I will hold my child, any child, close to me and I will explain that terrorism is being stalked and surveilled simply because you are alive. And terrorism is being put in solitary confinement and starved and beaten. And terrorism is not being able to feed your children despite working three jobs. And terrorism is not having a decent school or a place to play" (Khan-Cullors and Bandele 2017, p. 252). Linguistic disobedience demands that we reject labels that deny people's humanity, perpetuate dangerous myths or outright lies about marginalized peoples, or mislead listeners and readers about history. These efforts are not necessarily to convince others, though that possibility is unleashed each time we speak. Instead, we do these things to assert, over and over again, alternate visions of freedom, democracy, justice, and peace for ourselves and those willing to hear.

The Power(s) of Correction

In the aftermath of an alarmingly massive nationalist and far-right march in Poland in November 2017, veteran journalist Timothy Garton Ash enjoined "online platforms, public figures and everyday neighbours" to form a "popular front [...] against [the] mainstreaming of far-right language and ideas." Rather than leaving the work of correction to the powerful ("the platforms, the politicians, and the clerics"), he placed the onus on "you and me." He continued, "For nowadays we are all neighbours of people susceptible to such extreme views – if not physical neighbours, then certainly virtual ones. ... Every time we hear such views expressed, whether in the pub or the cafe, at the football ground or on Facebook, we need to speak up. It doesn't have to be angry polemic. It can also be ridicule. Humour is a great antidote to fanaticism" (Garton Ash 2017).

Ash is onto something here. His admonition that all of us must "speak up" against views we find abhorrent, and the words used to convey those views, complements the argument advanced in this chapter, that interruption and correction is a potent form of linguistic disobedience. And what of humor as a vehicle for challenging "fanaticism"? In his widely read 1968 study of "folk humor," Mikhail Bakhtin (1984, p. 12) noted its ambivalent property: laughter "asserts and denies, buries and revives." In the countless responses to Trumpspeak that have circulated this past year, some of the most satisfying have come from professional comics such as those who perform on *Saturday Night Live*, who have ruthlessly parodied not only Trump, but Sean Spicer, Sarah Huckabee Sanders, and others, mocking their mannerisms, their facial expressions, and yes, their language patterns and word choices. And out of many corners of the internet come memes, humorous commentaries, and screenshots that provide fleeting relief from the relentless swirl of bad news. The extent to which these circuits of humor reach anyone outside of our echo chambers (or even whether our echo chambers are detrimental or productive) is debatable, but it seems important to acknowledge that humor may indeed be a skill to cultivate as part of corrective efforts (Parker 2017).

Much virtual ink has been spilled on all the nefarious ways different forms of media are shaping political discourse. Still, in thinking about correction, it is hard not to celebrate the fact that a much wider range of corrections have been heard and seen because of social media. The "clap-back," now ensconced in everyday internet culture in the United States, is correction par excellence. Merriam-Webster's etymology of "clapback" traces its roots to hip-hop songs of the early 2000s, discovering that it refers to literal or metaphorical "return fire," or "responding to a criticism with a withering comeback." There is, of course, a violent element to reckon with here—"clap" referred originally to the sound of a gunshot. The clapback—the correction—is verbally lethal. And anyone can do it. African-American women politicians taking on the Trump administration across different forms of media, for example, have been a hallmark of 2017. Members of Congress Maxine Waters, Frederica Wilson, Karen Bass, and Ted Lieu have each made an art of correcting their political opponents in live interviews, tweets, and, most importantly perhaps, within the halls of Congress. Senator Elizabeth Warren's Twitter feed delivers stinging rebukes to Trump on a regular basis. In doing so, they set examples for how to do linguistic disobedience, blending immediacy, clarity, and correction, often with a healthy dose of humor.

But clapbacks, sarcasm, and humor will not be enough. What is needed is sustained attention to making corrections whenever and in whatever register they are required. In the United States, the quintessential space of conflict has become the Thanksgiving holiday dinner table. Family members with divergent political views choose not to discuss "politics" in order to keep the peace and enjoy pleasant gatherings. In classrooms, educators make daily decisions about whether and how to discuss current events topics with their students, not quite sure what might result in accusations of creating unsafe spaces, most recently, for conservative students. In everyday encounters in coffee shops, craft stores, supermarkets, and public transportation ordinary people have seen more and more verbal and physical aggressions driven by xenophobia, Islamophobia, and racism happen before their very eyes. In all of these cases, individuals must at a minimum assess the extent to which correction might cause damage to relationships or livelihoods. At worst, they must weigh the extent to which they are willing to put their bodies on the line to correct abuse unfolding in front of them. These are all personal decisions. But as more and more individuals recognize that correction is an expression of language ownership, and a scaffolding upon which to build resistance in everyday life, collective willingness to correct our authority figures, our fellow board members, our families, our friends, will grow.

Language warriors can reclaim words and concepts that have been bankrupted by misuse or absent historical context. When conservatives rail against the social safety net as "entitlements," linguistic disobedience pushes us to make a correction: people have paid for Social Security and Medicare their entire working lives, and the government has promised to care for retirees using those funds. When historically uninformed young families move into neighborhoods formerly inhabited by working-class black and brown people and celebrate "gentrification" as a good, linguistic disobedience enjoins us to call out the process for what it is: a continuation of entrenched patterns of failing to protect access to affordable housing from racist capitalism that views neighborhoods merely as real estate. When a police officer describes an unarmed African-American teenager like Michael Brown as a "demon," linguistic disobedience compels us to correct this characterization by showing that it is, in fact, a trope that has been used to characterize black men as monsters for centuries. It is our duty to make these corrections early, often, and with hope. In Solnit's words, "hope is only a beginning; it's not a substitute for action, only a basis for it" (Solnit 2016, p. xviii). Each time we make a correction we proceed another step along the path of struggle. "Things don't always change for the better," she writes, "but they change, and we can play a role in that change if we act" (xix). Or as Keeanga-Yamahtta Taylor notes with reference to the history and present of the quest for Black freedom, "No one knows what stage the current movement is in or where it is headed. [...] But we do know that there will be relentless efforts to subvert, redirect, and unravel the movement for Black lives, because when the Black movement goes into motion, it throws the entire mythology of the United States—freedom, democracy, and endless opportunity—into chaos" (Taylor 2016, p. 218). Linguistic disobedience corrects these mythologies because this work is "how we get free" (Taylor 2017).

Correction is generative. Each time we correct each other, we are creating new opportunities for redirecting political discourse and energy. The language of decolonization, as articulated by Ngũgĩ wa Thiong'o in the 1970s and 1980s has seeped into wider discourse, so that wider reading publics have the tools to discern that "settler" is not an innocent word, but one that contains violent meanings for indigenous peoples. Once one has this knowledge, it becomes impossible to ignore the many relentless and interlocking ways that "settler societies" have caused harm to indigenous peoples over centuries. The effort to defend Standing Rock in 2016 did not emerge from a void. Instead, it emerged from the activism of Native Americans who mobilized to defend their sacred lands from further capitalist encroachment. Interpreted through the lens of settler colonialism, with the masses of historical evidence that reveals this history in all of its gruesome detail, it becomes impossible to view the imposition of the Dakota Access Pipeline as anything other than a continuation and exacerbation of the United States' sordid history of violence against Native Americans.

Unsurprisingly, some of the most inspiring advocates for linguistic disobedience are revolutionaries. After all, their primary job is to inspire people to follow their radical visions. Thomas Sankara, the President of Burkina Faso (formerly Upper Volta) from 1983 to 1987, lived up to this name on a number of levels (Harsch 2014). He came to power in a military coup as a young army captain, but soon proved himself a singular revolutionary leader. He undertook numerous reforms to set Burkina Faso on a course toward reducing poverty, increasing access to education, and rejecting capitalist imperialism. Having adopted the new name of Burkina Faso—"the land of the upright people"—to replace the old colonial name of Upper Volta, its citizens, the Burkinabé, set about implementing Sankara's vision of equality by organizing "to carry out deep-going economic and social measures that curtailed the rights and prerogatives of the region's landed aristocracy and wealthy merchants" (Prairie 2007, p. 21) Under Sankara's leadership, Burkinabé achievements in redistributing farm land and wealth, improving the population's access to health and education, and building necessary infrastructure through public works, were nothing short of spectacular. Seeing the fate of the Burkinabé as linked to that of millions of others around the world, Sankara worked tirelessly to cultivate "internationalist solidarity with those fighting oppression and exploitation in Africa and worldwide" (p. 21).

Sankara was also a language warrior. He championed the idea espoused by Ngũgĩ that Africans should have opportunities to learn, read, write, and speak in their indigenous languages, though he also felt that French, the colonial language, had an important role to play in Burkinabé expression and in aiding international anti-imperial solidarity. In speeches at rallies in Burkina Faso, as well as in front of international bodies like the Organization of African Unity and the United Nations, Sankara returned time and again to core revolutionary ideals of self-help, equality for all, women's emancipation, and national sovereignty. He also practiced a level of correction that struck at the heart of the neocolonial structure when he stood in front of international bodies to make a case against African debt payments. He is worth quoting at length here:

> We believe analysis of the debt should begin with its roots. The roots of the debt go back to the beginning of colonialism. Those who lent us the money were those who colonized us. They were the same people who ran our states and our economies. It was the colonizers who put Africa into debt to the financiers—their brothers and cousins. This debt has nothing to do with us. That's why we cannot pay it. (Prairie 2007, p. 375)

Calling debt a "cleverly reorganized reconquest of Africa," he attempted to strike at the foundations of what had become the neocolonial order: banking entities like the International Monetary Fund (IMF) and World Bank, alongside aid coming from the wealthy North and other organizations, had undercut the ability of African nations to pursue independence on their own terms. Sankara kept up his revolutionary corrections until he was assassinated in 1987 by his opponents, the elite class who had lost their wealth to his experiment in socialism. Blaise Compaoré, who had helped bring Sankara to power in 1983 and then served as Minister of Defence, and who likely orchestrated Sankara's murder, ruled Burkina Faso for the better part of the next three decades (Zeilig 2015). Sankara's inspiration, however, lived on, sparking a new generation of Burkinabé to eventually rise up against Compaoré, ousting him from power and forcing him into exile in 2014. As with any iconic figure whose memory fires the imaginations of those who follow in their footsteps, Sankara's status as a hero is complex—after all, he came to power in a military coup—and there is room for "sympathetic critique" of his accomplishments and those of his fellow Burkinabé (Battistoli 2017). But his fierce dedication to issuing bold correctives to powerful and wealthy governments, banks, and international organizations for all to hear remains an exemplar of linguistic disobedience that is worth teaching, emulating, imbibing.

Another selection from a Sankara speech resonates especially well in this moment, when people wonder openly about the utility of talking to other people across vast, seemingly unbridgeable divides. Speaking from the Burkinabé context, in trying to translate his elite Marxist ideas into everyday practice, he recognized the challenges he faced:

> If the masses have trouble understanding, it's still our fault. We have to correct errors, be more precise, adapt ourselves to the masses, and not try to adapt the masses to our own desires and our own dreams. Revolutionaries are not afraid of their mistakes. They have the political courage to admit them publicly, because doing so means a commitment to correcting them and to doing better. (Prairie 2007, p. 399)

Make mistakes. Admit errors publicly. Correct them. Do better. We could do worse.

Notes

1. Frente de Libertação de Moçambique, or FRELIMO, was formed as a nationalist organization to fight against Portuguese colonial rule in what is today Mozambique. After the Portuguese withdrew from Mozambique in 1975, FRELIMO became the governing party. A long civil war (1976–1992) between FRELIMO and the opposition party RENAMO (Resistência Nacional Moçambicana), which was aligned with apartheid South Africa and white minority-ruled Rhodesia (now Zimbabwe), ensued.

2. For another example of a structural critique of racism delivered from within the carceral system, see George Jackson, *Soledad Brother: The Prison Letters of George Jackson* (Chicago: Lawrence Hill Books, 1994), 17–28.
3. See also Danticat, p. 11: "[C]reating as a revolt against silence, creating when both the creation and the reception, the writing and the reading, are dangerous undertakings, disobedience to a directive."
4. Compare Barber's "Fourteen Steps Forward Together" to Naomi Klein's "Leap Manifesto" in *No is Not Enough: Resisting Trump's Shock Politics and Winning the World We Need* (Chicago, IL: Haymarket, 2017), 267–271.
5. https://poorpeoplescampaign.org/.

References

Aizenman, Nurith. "Is It Insulting to Call This a Hut?" *NPR*, November 12, 2017. https://www.npr.org/sections/goatsandsoda/2017/11/12/563305753/is-it-insulting-to-call-this-a-hut.

Arendt, Hannah. *The Human Condition*. Chicago: The University of Chicago Press, 1958.

Bakhtin, Mikhail. *Rabelais and His World*. Translated by Helene Iswolsky. Bloomington: Indiana University Press, 1984.

Barber, Reverend William J. II, with Jonathan Wilson-Hartgrove. *The Third Reconstruction: How a Moral Movement Is Overcoming the Politics of Division and Fear*. Boston: Beacon Press, 2016.

Battistoli, D. S. "What Would a Sympathetic Critique of Thomas Sankara Look Like?" *Africa is a Country*, February 27, 2017. http://africasacountry.com/2017/02/what-would-a-sympathetic-critique-of-thomas-sankara-look-like/.

Biko, Steve. *I Write What I Like: A Selection of His Writings Edited with a Personal Memoir and a New Preface by Aelred Stubbs C.R.* San Francisco: Harper and Row, 1986.

Černý, Václav. "On the Question of Chartism." In *The Power of the Powerless*, edited by John Keane and translated by Paul Wilson. Armonk, NY: M. E. Sharpe, 1985.

Danticat, Edwidge. *Create Dangerously: The Immigrant Artist at Work*. New York: Vintage Books, 2011.

Faiola, Anthony and Stephanie Kirchner. "This German Reporter Took on Trump. Now She's Being Hailed at Home." *The Washington Post*, March 20, 2017.

Fallows, James. "A Nation of Tribes, and Members of the Tribes." *The Atlantic*, November 4, 2017. https://www.theatlantic.com/notes/2017/11/a-nation-of-tribes-and-members-of-the-tribe/544907/.

Garton Ash, Timothy. "Yes, We Can Halt the Rise of the International Far Right." *The Guardian*, November 17, 2017. https://www.theguardian.com/commentisfree/2017/nov/17/international-far-right-poland-march-nationalism.

Harsch, Ernest. *Thomas Sankara: An African Revolutionary.* Athens, OH: Ohio University Press, 2014.

Itkowitz, Colby. "Donald Trump Says We're All Too Politically Correct. But Is That Also a Way to Limit Speech?" *The Washington Post*, December 9, 2015. https://www.washingtonpost.com/news/inspired-life/wp/2015/12/09/donald-trump-says-were-all-too-politically-correct-but-is-that-also-a-way-to-limit-speech/?utm_term=.3ab9f8205ca3.

Jackson, George. *Soledad Brother: The Prison Letters of George Jackson.* Chicago: Lawrence Hill Books, 1994.

Jones, Hayley. "MSNBC Hosts Shut Down Trump Backer in Bonkers Interview: 'Fire Your Press Person!'" *The Daily Beast*, August 17, 2017. https://www.thedailybeast.com/msnbc-hosts-ali-velshi-stephanie-ruhle-brad-thomas-trump-interview.

Keith, Tamara and Amita Kelly. "Hillary Clinton's Three Word Misstep: 'All Lives Matter.'" *NPR*, June 24, 2015. https://www.npr.org/sections/itsallpolitics/2015/06/24/417112956/hillary-clintons-three-word-gaffe-all-lives-matter.

Keim, Curtis and Carolyn Somerville. *Mistaking Africa: Curiosities and Inventions of the American Mind*, 4th edition. New York: Westview Press, 2018.

Khan-Cullors, Patrisse and Asha Bandele. *When They Call You a Terrorist: A Black Lives Matter Memoir.* New York: St. Martin's Press, 2017.

Klein, Naomi. "Leap Manifesto." In *No Is Not Enough: Resisting Trump's Shock Politics and Winning the World We Need.* 267–271. Chicago: Haymarket Press, 2017.

Lalami, Laila. "Why Republicans Cry Political Correctness." *The Nation*, April 7, 2016. https://www.thenation.com/article/why-republicans-cry-political-correctness/.

Laymon, Kiese. *How to Slowly Kill Yourself and Others in America*. Chicago: Bolden, 2013.

Lee, Jarry. "14 Times the Merriam-Webster Dictionary was Shady AF." *Buzzfeed*, February 2, 2017. https://www.buzzfeed.com/jarrylee/14-times-the-merriam-webster-dictionary-was-shady-af?utm_term=.mp8JvnBvYZ#.upawAj1Aa4.

Lorde, Audre. *Sister Outsider*. Berkeley, CA: Crossing Press, 2007.

Makoni, Sinfree, Geneva Smitherman, Arnetha F. Ball, and Arthur K. Spears, eds. *Black Linguistics: Language, Society, and Politics in Africa and the Americas*. London: Routledge, 2002.

Mendoza, Samantha. "What Does Richard Spencer Want? The White Supremacist Leader Led the Latest Charlottesville Rally." *Bustle*, October 8, 2017. https://www.bustle.com/p/what-does-richard-spencer-want-the-white-supremacist-leader-led-the-latest-charlottesville-rally-2810607.

Merriam-Webster.com. Accessed December 17, 2017. https://www.merriam-webster.com/.

Mozur, Paul. "A Reporter Rolled Her Eyes, and China's Internet Broke." *The New York Times*, March 13, 2018.

Ngũgĩ wa Thiong'o. *Decolonising the Mind: The Politics of Language in African Literature*. London: James Currey, 1986.

Ngugi, Mukoma wa. "What *Decolonising the Mind* Means Today." *Literary Hub*, March 23, 2018. https://lithub.com/mukoma-wa-ngugi-what-decolonizing-the-mind-means-today/#_ftnref6.

Parker, Emily. "In Praise of Echo Chambers." *The Washington Post*, May 22, 2017. https://www.washingtonpost.com/news/democracy-post/wp/2017/05/22/in-praise-of-echo-chambers/?utm_term=.f694438a2a92.

Prairie, Michael, ed. *Thomas Sankara Speaks: The Burkina Faso Revolution 1983–1987*. London: Pathfinder, 2007.

"Poor Peoples' Campaign: A National Call for Moral Revival." https://poorpeoplescampaign.org/.

Shribman, David M. "Yes, the Truth Still Matters." *The New York Times*. December 11, 2017.

Simons, Gary F. and Charles D. Fennig, eds. *Ethnologue: Languages of the World, Twenty-First Edition*. Dallas, TX: SIL International, 2018. Online version: http://www.ethnologue.com.

Solnit, Rebecca. *Hope in the Dark: Untold Histories, Wild Possibilities*. Chicago: Haymarket Press, 2016.

Tannen, Deborah. "New York Jewish Conversational Style." *International Journal of the Sociology of Language* 30 (1981): 133–149.

Taylor, Keeanga-Yamahtta. *From #BlackLivesMatter to Black Liberation.* Chicago: Haymarket Press, 2016.

Taylor, Keeanga-Yamahtta. *How We Get Free: Black Feminism and the Combahee River Collective.* Chicago: Haymarket Press, 2017.

ten Thije, Jan D. and Ludger Zeevawert, eds. *Receptive Multilingualism: Linguistic Analyses, Language Policies and Didactic Concepts.* Amsterdam: John Benjamins, 2007.

Wainaina, Binyavanga. "How to Write About Africa." *Granta* 92 (2006). https://granta.com/how-to-write-about-africa/.

"What's a Clapback?" Merriam-Webster.com. https://www.merriam-webster.com/words-at-play/clapback-meaning-origin.

Yıldız, Yasemin. *Beyond the Mother Tongue: The Postmonolingual Condition.* New York: Fordham University Press, 2012.

Zeilig, Leo. "The Murder of Thomas Sankara: October 15, 1987" *Africa Is a Country.* October 15, 2015. http://africasacountry.com/2015/10/the-murder-of-thomas-sankara/.

4

Care

The kind of linguistic disobedience that can restore power to civic language requires from us, too, a new vision of *care for language*—as a complex and common good. As Marilyn Chandler McEntyre puts it, "Like any other life-sustaining resource, language can be depleted, polluted, contaminated, eroded, and filled with artificial stimulants. Like any other resource, it needs the protection of those who recognize its value and commit themselves to good stewardship" (2009, p. 1). But just making sure our own contributions to a given conversation are astute, clever, on-point, timely, clear, and precise is, though impressive as a linguistic feat, not quite the same as caring for language. On the social journey of critiquing and correcting our own ever-next formulations of meaning in the world, we also need to carry with us a resolute decision to favor, rather than fear, the overall endeavor of human speaking. To like, indeed to love, language—especially when, as Rebecca Traister beautifully puts it, "The anger window is open" (2017). To consider language beloved, regardless of what our paying vocations might tell us about it, or how our language repertoires might be most readily described in economic or institutional terms. To be an amateur in it, with it, around it. This decision, too, is a form of linguistic disobedience, in a historical age that

Y. Komska et al., *Linguistic Disobedience*,
https://doi.org/10.1007/978-3-319-92010-8_4

105

presumes fear of language as the more likely and rational choice: fear, justified or not, of the ever-imminent distortion, misappropriation, surveilling, forensic capture, monetization, or dispossession of our or others' living language.

If, faced with all these ready-made reasons our age has given us to feel risk-averse toward language use in civic life, we find we just cannot intuitively come to like language(s) as such, then we can still perhaps begin by making a decision to favor language—as it exists in the mouths of our treasured elders, children, truth-tellers, mentors, co-strangers, and artists. Even, and maybe especially, when we don't quite feel we understand the words they're saying, or singing, in our midst. Listening to language is indeed something more than just deciphering meanings, and speaking is something more, too, than merely "what you bring to the table." Such neoliberal discourses of competitive excellence, ego-pragmatism, and incessant self-distinction seem designed to put all kinds of language-makers (whether at work or at leisure) ever behind the eight-ball of communicative activity. Leveraged to the hilt by late capitalism, twenty-first-century conversationalists may vaguely, or acutely, sense some of the ways in which older conversational resources of play, irony, ambiguity, shade, hedging, and excess are being crowded out of talk by the property grabs of hot-takes, relatability, talking-points, product placement, and unique-selling-points. Disciplined by such a pressing economy of talk, we command ourselves and others to "make no mistake"; we entreat others to "let me be clear"; we banish ambivalence and counterevidence to the slush pile of our thought. Even intimate conversation is not immune to such actuarial technologization and industrialization from without, as novels like Sarah Schulman's *The Mere Future* (2011) have attested.

But communicative competence is ultimately not, we think, the cardinal virtue when it comes to having a satisfying relationship to language in the world; sometimes agreeing for a moment just to love and favor language's unruly plentitude in our midst—and to do so rudimentarily, partially, and without any view to mastery—can nourish an enduring daily care for language better than systematic analysis could.

Deficit models that quietly intimate to young adults that their language is somehow too inarticulate, too compliant, too fashionable, too unfashionable, too regional, too ethnic, or not "appropriate for the global workplace" will most likely dissuade them from being able to like language at all, ever—theirs or anyone else's. Touting globe-trotting multilingualism on glossy brochures as the ticket out of an austerity economy will most likely make those same young people feel low-key shame, if not reactionary disdain, toward the 7000 other planetary languages they or their parents may not have had time, money, or prompting to "immerse" themselves in. And being "stingy with language" (Phipps 2017, p. 99)—hoarding or saving particular prestige registers, repertoires, and sometimes whole languages for a select few addressees in our lives—is a sure-fire way to monoculture our linguistic landscapes into unarability and peoplelessness. To re-embark earnestly on care for language in civic life, we need to come face-to-face with the forms of linguaphobia that capitalism, patriarchy, neoliberalism, and raciolinguistics have rendered so normal in our places of dwelling and working that we never quite knew they were part of our experience to begin with (Flores and Rosa 2015).

When it comes to language care, there is simply so much room to grow—and so much meaning to "rewild," as the applied linguist Steve Thorne (2018) hopefully suggests. Young people can be taught in their public schools how to love their own species' language(s) affectionately, in the way that they already quite effortlessly love watching birds or flowers or snakes or elephants do extraordinary and perplexing things around each other. It can be pointed out to preschoolers, very early on in their linguistic lives, that social contempt arising from the "opacity of style"— as Deborah Tannen (1981, p. 144) described humans' near-universal tendency to misinterpret the linguistic choices of others, due to our unfamiliarity with how meaning works in their neighborhood—can and must be overcome in any democracy that desires to remain one. Cultivating such a practical ethics around social and stylistic opacity in our affairs is not some facile dodge toward relativism; it is a decision to recognize, or to cease misrecognizing, a complex anthropological feature of everyone's everyday lives.

In middle school, high school, or college, students of the most varied linguistic and vocational orientations can be trained, in writing or "language arts" courses, how to record, transcribe, and analyze the speech of their peer groups—not in order to fix anything or address any inadequacies, but to highlight how exactly it is that these young people make sense together in their own communities and spaces, using subtle resources that outsiders (adults, teachers, politicians, and language purists) fail to grasp or admire. Students who learn these things can, of course, become professional applied linguists later—but they can also, with these empirically engaged language insights, become social workers, chefs, vet techs, law enforcement officers, drag performers, union organizers, casting agents, civil engineers, band leaders, public administrators, preachers, and other workers-among-workers. With a little persistence, we can convince young people who "translanguage" furtively among and around diplomatically recognizable "languages," like French and Arabic and English and ASL, that they indeed do this not at the expense of the integrity of those languages, or out of a lack of mastery of them, but as an act of ambitious meaning-making and expert ingenuity, the likes of which our planet may have never yet seen (Li Wei 2017; Canagarajah 2011). *All* young people can be convinced that they, too, are always potentially on the verge of an epic win in language use: a social moment, any moment, where they will have combined words in a way that soothes suffering, or honors experience, or invests in complexity, or interrupts a mobbing, or extends a "vision of sanity" (Tannen 1981) to someone who may, half-knowingly, desperately need one. This, we believe, is "presidential behavior."

Such a magical and inexpensive offering in everyday language use can be as concrete as respectfully repeating a beloved (though not necessarily a high-profile) word from another's discourse or prior turn-at-talk—of deciding to "say her name" for instance—when doing so somehow seems not quite interactionally required, given the presumed pragmatic conventions of the setting. For human speakers of all backgrounds and dispositions, it is often a frustrating anthropological predicament to be unable, in any given situation, to get particular words to come out of others' mouths—much to the acute disappointment of lazy, powerful authoritarians.

And so when we do conscientiously choose to put others' subtly treasured words in our own mouths, this *can* be an act of uniquely surprising generosity, rather than of careless appropriation. Care for language of this sort occurs in hallways, at photocopiers, on customer-care lines, in shared ride vehicles, in the aisles of over-packed regional jets, in line at the Social Security administration, and while playing Massive Multiplayer Online Games. Care in language can be taken in situations of radical discursive asymmetry, in the midst of complex relations of power and distance, in service encounters, on first or last dates, while teaching or learning, with strangers and with intimates, with people whose languages we don't know and with people who helped us get language in the first place. Care is not a transaction; it is not a means to "add value" to a semiotic commodity, nor to engender a certain social result. Caring for language simply expresses the desire for a transformational dimensionality in everyday meaning, a dimensionality which no institution or order can comfortably imagine on its own. Forerunners in this line of thinking, now 50 years hence, were courageous feminist anthropologists, poets, theologians, psychologists, nurses, and educators, who saw an ethics of care as requiring an entirely "different voice" in language and civic life (Gilligan 1982; Watson 1979).

But, actually, caring for language costs little in the way of extra time or money. The catch is that it most often does mean abandoning interactional advantage—or at least those forms of interactional advantage that we may be most spontaneously expected to value in the current age, given our presumed identity investments. Social supremacy and interactional advantage are to language care what crop-dusters are to wildflowers. Institutional cultures that have, for one reason or another, doggedly attuned themselves to the rationality of social advantage are likely to have very little extra square-footage left over for joy and care around the human use of languages. Like the Vacant City above New York, where 250,000 apartments sit unused in a megalopolis that desperately needs affordable housing, austerity economies tend also to force certain kinds of language out of public intelligibility and into silent indefiniteness. Against the backdrop of our present-day audit culture's spectrum of virtues and vices, choosing to cede interactional advantage is essentially the linguistic equivalent of taking a stock loss in a delusional bull market. Guileless as it may seem in a financially rationalized culture, caring for language is menacingly beyond the reach of financial logics. It's an always-available stance, a qualitatively different way of relating to the present, a way of opening an easy door to a complex potential transformation of the social world. But caring for language requires of us, and then offers back to us, renewed intensities of awareness toward features of human language that—from Descartes to the Frankfurt School, and certainly today in the age of big-data harvesting and algorithmic translatability—have always had a hard time finding relevance in the analytical frame: the embodied, the nonpropositional, the nonconceptual, the prosodic, the material, the gestural, the poetic, the interactional, the paralinguistic, the spontaneous, the abortive, the irrelevant, the disorderly, the loud, the silent, and the noncommunicative. To care for language in our times, we will need to give freely to it of our trust, strength, experience, permission to roam, and affection, such that when, in Lucille Clifton's words, our civic language is again "strong enough to travel on her own, beware, she will" (2015 [1991]).

Rewilding the Modern Object of Language

As our previous chapters suggested, there is some serious, meaningful, and—we think—exciting tension between these core activities of care, critique, and correction in language. Centuries of institutional work to correct and rationalize the civic use of language among domesticated populations have long lent zealous, exacting attention to language as a *Gegenstand*. This German word for "object," literally meaning "stands against," illustrates a thing that stands against or in opposition to the observer/agent. Treating language like something that stands in opposition to us, and that can or must be trained to serve us better, tends to set up schemas in which languages in turn become feared, dominated, and guarded against. But just as plausible and pragmatic, we think, is a stance of sensuously enacting language(s) as a worldly and human predicament to be cherished, inhabited, and trusted—just as well as one can cherish, inhabit, and trust anything else in the world.

Since the seventeenth century, our academic and political institutions have, with their own good intentions, tinkered, blasted, shaped, scoured, purified, squared off, and sharpened that *civic* object called Language (and not just *scholastic* and *sacred* languages, which elites had always zealously honed in premodern ages), such that modern languages—and official characterizations of them—are in practice no longer much like what they had been in the fifteenth century. But all of this deliberate work on the object of standard secular language—identifying it, corralling it, disciplining it, disambiguating it, and sentencing it—has not necessarily made human beings much more capable of caring for one another in language, or for caring for language itself, in the broad senses of "care" and "language" alike.

But there's a further problem. Historically, "care of language"—or *Sprachpflege* in the German tradition—has most often been a darling of the nationalist, guarding an idealized and often violently coerced standard cultural variant of a language against incursions from outside and below. This tradition of "care for language" lends *Sprachpflege* a rather dubious, if not flat-out racist, relation to the possibility of caring in any non-national or ethnically agnostic way about how humans make their meaning in language. Neither is there a whole lot of evidence that care over the last five centuries—in the form of linguistic rationalism, ethnic romanticism, or planned monolingualism—has led to a world in which humans communicate about that world better, refer to it more accurately, or engage it more justly (Stibbe 2015). Such ethical projects, of course, are not the same in their scope or ends as the sociopolitical projects of cultivating a middle-class, nurturing the autonomy of erudite elites, propagating national cultural traditions, or globalizing the free market, though these efforts have always been intertwined with linguistic care of some sort. So how has the treatment of language as a domesticated object affected us and our cultures? How is it affecting them now?

Indeed, little has changed in the grand scheme of the "global language system" (de Swaan 2001) since seventeenth-century linguists in France and Britain decided that free people needed rational, purified, and transparent repertoires of common reference, proposition, and cognition, labeled always according to one roughly singular ethnicity or nation. The notion that every citizen-subject who sought individuality, success, and insight needed one of these improved and sanctioned "national languages" (and one only) persisted deep into postcolonial language planning efforts of the 1960s and 1970s (Ricento 2000). Subsequently, since the 1980s, these hard-won monolanguages have been subject to ever more actuarial "clarification," according to the shifting needs of globalized free-market late capitalism (Duchêne and Heller 2012; Cameron 2008), lest complex and unruly human multilingualism itself "balkanize the information space" (Oard 2006, p. 299) to the detriment of the orderly international flow of symbolic commodities. But throughout these modern transformations, language has not itself been the beneficiary of much *care*.

In his 2016 book *Banking on Words,* the anthropologist Arjun Appadurai has gone so far as to claim that "the failure of the financial system in 2007–8 in the United States was primarily a failure of language." The functional integrity of the linguistic form of the *promise*, so Appadurai explains, had been fundamentally hijacked by the discourse of traders, despite their hyperrational traffic *about* financial promises. Language, he believes, was in fact *the* primary domain in which the financial collapse was perpetrated—rather than, say, the moral or actuarial domains most routinely invoked in critical commentaries on stock-trading: "This argument does not deny that greed, ignorance, weak regulation, and irresponsible risk-taking were important factors in the collapse. But the new role of language in the marketplace is the condition of possibility for all these more easily identifiable flaws" (Appardurai 2016, p. 1). This is a stunning claim for many of us who have grown up more or less expecting to hear every new day about unbridled capitalist greed in our midst. Attuned as citizens are to finding moral flaws in big business and privatized governance, we are often at a loss for describing the ways in which language itself has been refunctionalized by those sectors to systematically fail *us*— in various circumstances of urgency, trust, and need. What happens when too-big-to-fail languages—like the emptied-out English of international finance circa 2007—are propped up by plutocrats, despite having no real-world referent left to speak of, circling around nothing but "that void at the heart of the translating system" (Lezra 2015, p. 176).

Care and Ambivalence

Perhaps Appadurai's argument about the failure of the linguistic form of the promise in the Great Recession of 2008 shows that only a structural failure (internal or external) can bring societies to take interest in the functioning of their language, while only near socio-economic collapse might raise the general will to investigate it fully and honestly, as we suggested in our chapter on critique. So what gets done to civic language in those gray seasons when we are not prompted to care for it, and what does it look like when we indeed choose to do so nonetheless?

In *Caring for Words in a Culture of Lies* (2009), the medical humanist and literary comparatist Marilyn Chandler McEntyre offers an image of language as something that needs care and, particularly, stewardship. It can be polluted, she suggests, as water and air can be polluted. In the contemporary swarm of identities, politics, desires, media cycles, and shock events, civic language can become fatigued and devalued to such an extent that those who use it barely recognize its existence (despite using it all along!), or they recognize it only when it gets out of control, or out of order. In this way, care often runs up against similar roadblocks as do critique and correction. Indeed, commenting about language occurs customarily when something about it has become a problem, for one reason or another. "Language!" complains a parent, at wit's end with her swearing teenager. Or "Such *language* is unbecoming an officer of the court," admonishes a judge. Or we, rolling up our language-critical sleeves, see fit to bemoan jargon, blather, nonsense, shlock, banter, chattiness, mincing words, mealy-mouthedness, drivel, and gossip. Turn-of-the-millennium television programs like *The West Wing* (directed by Aaron Sorkin) schooled a generation of viewers, among other things, on how and why to be hypervigilant about the damning consequences of these wayward forms of language in political life, but also how and why to deploy them most effectively.

Under global free-market late capitalism, language has appeared to be an elusive item—no longer merely a badge of pride, but not yet a stable conveyer of profit (Duchêne and Heller 2012). Hard to monetize, financialize, and securitize, despite increasingly vigorous efforts to do so, language does not obey most of the customary prerequisites of commodity formation, nor the supply-side manufacture logistics procedures that convey commodities to end users (Pym 2004). An ambivalently valued half-commodity/half-commonwealth, language tends to be thematized in geo-political discourse only when it becomes inflamed or problematic.

But language also always gives us, when held at the right angle, an acute and consciousness-raising image of our relative distance to truth, joy, accuracy, sanity, alienation, peoplelessness, and worldedness. Marilyn Chandler McEntyre's underlying metaphor—of language as a natural, ideally healthy resource—is however only a partial story, a charismatic story indeed, but one that creates as many new problems as it identifies. We know from our own experiences that language is not *just* good language, appropriate language, beautiful language, friendly language, accurate language, or articulate language. It is not necessarily at its best when it is being nice, or benign, or nourishing, or productive. Precise, silver-tongued language can be the most violent language. Relatable, fluent language can be sociopathic. Charismatic, folksy language can become genocidal language from one phrase to the next. Idioms of intimacy can careen into idioms of misogyny before anyone has a chance to notice. So-called native-speaker language can be the most tone-deaf of all to creativity, poiesis, and the illusive mechanics of power.

Like all resources, whether human-made or mined from the earth, language is in the last instance a troublingly neutral, strangely textured, functionally multivalent, undomesticated, and unredeemed phenomenon. An ecological complexity rather than an object or subject, "it" has never promised us anything, in quite the ways securities traders promise each other higher and higher dividends. Humans have tried hard to bend it and make it work for us and for our moral and economic projects. More even, perhaps, than in the case of water or air—we feel somehow that it belongs to us by right, that we are its parent, and that we are responsible for it, as we suggested in the introduction. Animals and inanimate beings are rarely dragged into our human debates about good and bad language, unless—on the rare occasion—that language is seen as good or bad because it misrepresents those beings, or renders them invisible altogether (Stibbe 2015).

Generations of prescriptivist approaches to language have tried and tried to change language itself, to change how people use it, and to change the people whose language use we don't particularly like or understand. This underlying idea that we *can* change language has led, perhaps ironically, to a great deal of what the French linguist Philippe Blanchet (2016) calls "glossophobia," or fear of language. Fear of vague language, fear of propagandistic language, fear of loud language, fear of underdeveloped language, fear of secret, foreign language being whispered ("about us!") on the train.

In the seventeenth century, grammarians began to fear the excesses of everyday language, as secular ideas began to replace theological accounts of where language came from and what it referred to. If language actually ultimately came from God, there was little to worry about. But as soon as language was understood, in modernity, as representing (human-made) realities and perceptions, rather than divine order—well, then, controlling language became understood as a way to control humans and their behavior too. Excesses like loudness, lewdness, exaggeration, immoderation, irrationality, political revolt, moral torpor, femininity, and other kinds of wayward mayhem would best be controlled, so these grammarians thought, by orderly, monolingual, rational, national, individual languages that brought with them a particular civic disposition for their emerging citizenry. The more orderly, rational, and well-installed the language, the fewer problems the population would present. Teaching these orderly and rational languages to entire domestic populations, in their literate and orthographic forms, became a major undertaking for eighteenth-century civil society, for subjugating newly colonized peoples in the nineteenth century, and for postcolonial nation-building projects in the mid-twentieth century. What seventeenth-century linguists called linguistic rationality, nineteenth- and twentieth-century nation-builders developed further in the form of Language Policy and Planning (Ricento 2000).

For five centuries now, monolingualism has served as the preferred vessel for care of language. One of the (themselves utterly multilingual) inventors of modern monolingualism had the following to say, for instance, about how one should write and speak when at one's best: "If in poetry, thought and expression are so tightly interlinked: then I must doubtlessly write in that language in which I have the highest authority, and power over the words, the broadest knowledge, or at least certainty that my boldness is not yet lawlessness: and this is undoubtedly the mother tongue" (Herder 1985–2000, p. 407; translation by Dembeck 2017, p. 4). So, even amid the creative and expressive use of language, eighteenth-century thinkers were highly concerned about orderlessness and chaos, which might undermine or even destroy the possibility of boldness, power, and truth in language. The main specter haunting modern uses of language was excess and lawlessness. Obviating these—we might even call them the joint specter of early modern "linguistic disobedience"—was postulated as the best and only way toward potentially cultivating ideals like truth, reason, civilization, and indeed beauty. If this sounds like an utterly colonial gesture to you, perhaps it is.

Many of us, especially those who write books, are deeply grateful for our ability to create somewhat orderly, literate texts, to use punctuation and orthography in effective ways befitting our particular communicative setting and situation. It is hard for us to see that our individual abilities to do so are part of any ongoing colonial scheme that has hurt, killed, reeducated, abjected, annihilated, or dismissed the value of so many other people's language(s). Many of us who build our lives around writing feel most free and most alive when we are building sensible sentences, often monolingual ones, which may or may not be beautiful to others—others who may or may not write or talk like us. That the history of (our) literacy is also the history of (our) racialization and of the violence of (our) empires is a terrible fact. Its stain on language reminds us that the ways we come to acquire our symbolic resources—linguistic competence, articulacy, style, intuitions—are never private, individual affairs. They are (trans)civic achievements: just as much a part of planetary political violence over centuries as they are fruits of our own childhood work in our local schools. This reality does not jibe, however, with received paradigms of language as something *internal, inherent,* and *individual* (sometimes referred to in shorthand as the "3I model" of linguistics, Steffensen 2015). To adequately understand how language is implicated in the complex experience of a shared world, we need to care for language under a broader model, along the lines of what the Danish linguist Sune Vork Steffensen (2015, p. 105), among others, has called a 4E model of language. Never merely residing within individuals, their inborn intellectual faculties, or abstract systems, language is and has always been something *embodied, ecological, extended,* and *enacted.*

Such a shift in models is as difficult for language specialists to take up as it is for anyone else, and the tendency in academic scholarship and in advanced expository writing communities to see in linguistic exactitude a particular private moral or political virtue is as understandable as it is alarming. As we get farther and farther along in our careers, we writers often tend to become ever more devout toward editorial precision. We develop subjectivities in writing that are moved by the smallest detail of style. We feel these matter, and we like to share that feeling with others. We honor the difference between "farther" and "further," between em dashes and en dashes; we care about whether a certain gerundial formulation causes an ambiguity of meaning that is too unstable to let lie, we reach the limits of our always undone language and we look around, gratefully. This is not just an egotistical exercise in correctness or mannerism; it is its own kind of cosmology, with a caliber of feeling befitting any theology. It unleashes, as we write, a dynamic aesthetic sense of care that, on our best days, we can feel ascending, slipping, or growing.

But this privately cultivated language is not necessarily a viable civic language, and its principles and experiences alone cannot be good guides to civic interaction, without "taking the long way around" first. It is the long way around to which this chapter about care is dedicated—one in which the avid language-lover first empties herself out, station by station, not only of the most egregious and inhuman forms of linguistic prescriptivism she may privately hold but also of the most subtle and tempting ones. This orientation might be called radical descriptivism, except that it is not committed to disregarding norms so much as to seeing local norms as an essential part of the linguistic traffic in meaning (Pratt 2002). This process of becoming primarily an interlocutor, subject to the words of others, rather than just the self-cultivating speaker or critic, is the process through which care for language can go from the scholastic to the civic, from the pedantic to the dynamic, and from the contemplative to the active. Certainly, spiritual leaders—pastors, monks, nuns, imams, and abbots—have come to know about this need, long before academics in fields like ethnomethodology, sociology of language, folkloristics, Conversation Analysis, and Ordinary Language Philosophy began to apprehend it systematically in the 1960s and 1970s.

Since then, however, it has only become more clear that language continues to be a tool of domination and that, if language is bending toward justice, is a strange historical arc indeed. Deborah Cameron's influential *Verbal Hygiene* (1995) and *Good to Talk: Living and Working in a Communication Culture* (2000) have offered dramatic evidence of the augmented role afforded to linguistic prescriptivism in contemporary social life. According to Cameron, "linguistic bigotry is among the last publicly expressible prejudices left to members of the western intelligentsia. Intellectuals who would find it unthinkable to sneer at a beggar [...] will sneer without compunction at linguistic 'solecisms'" (1995, p. 12). Nelson Flores and Jonathan Rosa (2015) have identified how appropriateness-based competence training in language education over recent decades has introduced new forms of "raciolinguistic" ideology into the learning experience of young people of color in US schools. Any approach to care of language has to contend primarily with these emergences, rather than beginning with the romantic metaphors of purity that guided twentieth-century *Sprachpflege*.

Care and Impurity

Returning to Chandler McEntyre's metaphor of language as healthy, nourishing resource worthy of stewardship, we might then notice that there is a looming conflict. Despite many a purist's obsession with terroir, the language we have been able to produce for ourselves, our relations, and our communities—whether expressive, sensible, meaningful, or beautiful language—is never quite homegrown. It's never straight from the garden, and even when it appears to be straight from the garden, that garden is on land taken from others long ago or recently, compromised by chemicals and erosion, and housing an unwieldy variety of species and substances transplanted over the last centuries from around the world. It is a recklessly extravagant, gorgeously superdiverse garden—enmeshed upward, downward, laterally, and inwardly. Such is ever the case with modern language—whose mixedness, compromised nature, and history of violence is no more intuitive to grasp and comfortable to acknowledge than that of the soil in our backyard. And yet language can be subjected to no chemical or genetic testing, in the way that soil samples can be. Though we love to spin etymological yarns about where words come from and how they take root in a place, words are like ancient inherited utensils—full of the marks and blemishes accrued from the work they have done, but often inscrutable when it comes to ascertaining how, where, by whom, and why they first made meaning in the way they do for us now.

Consider the Holocaust survivor and Italian Jewish chemist Primo Levi, one of the millions of those who have sustained crushing, long-term violence at the hands of the twentieth-century's purist authoritarian states. Levi once shared a surprising assessment about why he likes translating the writing of the multilingual Czech-Jewish-German writer Franz Kafka. Levi admits that:

> I love and admire Kafka because he writes in a way that is totally unavailable to me. In my writing, for good or evil, knowingly or not, I've always strived to pass from the darkness into light, as [...] a filtering pump might do, which sucks up turbid water and expels it decanted: possibly sterile. Kafka forges his path in the opposite direction: he endlessly unravels the hallucinations that he draws from incredibly profound layers, and he never filters them. The reader feels them swarm with germs and spores: they are gravid with burning significances, but he never receives any help in tearing through the veil or circumventing it to go and see what it conceals. (Gaeta 1983, n.p.)

A person who has endured such brutality at the hands of totalitarian culture would be justified perhaps in insisting on "admiring" only that language which clarifies, nourishes, and critically debunks. But this is not Levi's position, quite: though Levi himself does not and cannot write in the turbid, dark language of Kafka, he is able, in a sustained way, to care for this turbidity in others' work and words nonetheless. In the current moment—which has so dreadfully much in common with so many other dark, hopeless, enraged moments in human history—we can draw on Levi's learned and humbled insight about how to love others' language, no matter what that language's symbolic implications may be for one's own lived experience. Not just decanted, purified language deserves Levi's attention, but language that swarms, burns, infects, hallucinates, and obscures. Levi insists here that both kinds of language are worth admiration and care. He does not immunize or qualify his admiration for Kafka, by way of some critical, moral claim about what Kafka's language reveals about the banalities or evils of turn-of-the-century Prague. Such a moral justification of linguistic turbidity and toxicity—based for instance in Kafka's authorial aura, his intentionality, or his critical stance—is not necessary or even appropriate in Levi's estimation. Appropriate and necessary, instead, is an admiration without justification—a care of the language of this world. Levi's course in linguistic admiration is a kindred one to much research in Second Language Studies that emphasizes the anthropological import of the fact that humans can understand vastly more forms of language than they themselves can produce.

Levi brings us back from our closet crypto-prescriptivisms to a language world that is never pure, never unambiguously healthy, never quite good for us, never on the side of the angels, never just—just a world of language. People use language to gain and maintain power over others. People use it to lie and deceive, to obscure truth and history, to silence or shame others, to gain interactional prowess and advantage, to bellyache and fault-find, and to overemphasize the positive. Language belongs as much to them in those moments as it does to any critic on hand to behold them. And, as Chandler McEntyre tells us, we must care for it all. And we must see in the matrix of those utterances the immediate potential for all of the things we may desperately want: whether justice, truth, joy, beauty, righteousness, survival, whimsy, liberation, mindfulness, solidarity, divinity, friendship, expression, or disobedience.

With all of these demands placed upon language, though, it becomes almost seemingly natural that we would fear, resent, or seek to control language's consequences and range. It is exponentially more common in modern liberal societies to see legislative and judicial efforts to discourage certain kinds of language use than it is to encounter efforts to *promote* language use. Most US-based juridical decisions about "free speech" since the 1910s have focused on how to draw the line between what should and should not be said, rather than, say, on how to better enfranchise those who live in the United States to cultivate their freedom in language generally, openly, and publicly. High school and college students—indeed working adults, too—often import these ambient juridical strictures around "free speech" into their linguistic-interactional lives whole, without reflecting on the fact that the US First Amendment protecting against the "abridg[ing]" of speech by Congress applies to legislative, commercial, and political affairs, not to the private or semi-public realm of talk. Conversational interactions are then mistakenly, if idealistically, made to proceed according to a principle of "rights" that is awkward and ungermane in the everyday interactional realm.

For its part, the discipline of linguistics has studiously abstained from questions of "good" versus "bad" language since the 1950s (Cameron 1995). An important exception has been the field of Language Planning and Policy which, throughout the 1960s and 1970s, sought to shape "developing" languages to fit the modernist nationalist monolingualist models of what "a" language was expected to be, a model hegemonically taken as a given in Western European and US American contexts (Ricento 2000). The subsequent 20 years of postmodern thinking about language since 1980 have seen, in turn, a shift in perceptions on language-as-resource from an affirmative model of prestige, heritage, and distinction to the speculative model of commodity-trading (Bourdieu 2015; Katznelson and Bernstein 2017). Under late globalization regimes, language (in the sense of nationalized and standardized languages) has been transformed from a personal characteristic or talent to a acquirable and tradeable asset, subject to all of the manhandling that "being on the market" involves. Capitalism is catching up with language, quickly (Duchêne and Heller 2012; Cameron 2008).

Amid these transformations, it becomes ever more important to be clear about what *caring* for language entails—about the scope, scale, and relational settings in which care is to be pursued. Unlike tending a garden, for which one can don specific clothing, bring out the tools, and kneel down into the work at a specific time of day, caring for language is a stance so potentially ubiquitous and omnidirectional that it could quickly exhaust the imagination, the mind, the voice, and the body that undertakes it. When thinking back to Orwell's simple directive that we must "start at the verbal end," it is important to bear in mind the key word *start*.

Making a start into the care of language is the crucial threshold we need to cross each moment, and to be crossing always. Starting to care for language does not augur triumph, promise, or even competence at doing so—just a stance of decisiveness.

In the remainder of this chapter, we suggest a general scope of caring for language that is something other than stewardship, purification, or even observership, and that—in its resistance to received (nationalist, monolingualist) models of language care, is keyed toward linguistic disobedience in our time. Rather than being watchful and critical in a stationary way, the stance we suggest is agnostic, relational, free, relaxed, hospitable, nimble, and anticipatory—one that is more invested in caring for the space between speakers than in their performances as such. We will build this suggestion from the simplest impulse—"Care for language"—to the most complex form we find reasonable, if—at Orwell's urging—we intend to "start at the verbal end" of civic life. We lay out this cumulative suggestion in verse (or, perhaps, prayer) form, since the simplest ideas often need a special kind of format to stick:

> Make a decision
> to care for language
> as it is used
> in human and nonhuman interaction
> in complex, multilayered ways
> in times of great need
> and spaces of great suffering
> whether this language
> is an act of labor, work,
> leisure, pleasure,
> Or something else.

In these concluding sections of the chapter we try to sketch out what each of these clauses means to us, how it might conflict with received understandings of "caring for language," and how such a commitment may indeed form a principled basis for linguistic disobedience. Most of these clauses foreground situations of language *use* over the putative caliber and quality of language *usage*, suggesting that it may ultimately not be possible to care for language in any decontextualized way, without recognizing the always acute and local settings in which it moves us and others. But we begin with the elusive proposition that we should, in fact, *care for language.*

Care for Language

Abstract and foreboding as this thought is, it seems to leave us almost immediately blind-sided. Am I supposed to care for Donald Trump's language? Am I supposed to care for sexist, boorish, colonial language as it is used by people who have always enjoyed the power and privilege to dilate into whatever dominant idiom suits them in a given moment? Am I supposed to care for the neoliberal language of innovation, challenges, opportunity, creative disruption, responsibility, and excellence-through-competition, despite the fact that these idioms have hollowed out public institutions while purporting to reinvigorate them? Caring for these languages seems to be too big of an ask. But if I care instead for my own little patch of language—the poets I admire, the ironies and innuendos my friends and I use to get by and stay sane, the sharp-tongued critiques I leverage to indicate my dissent, the sardonic insider-talk podcasts I listen to while walking around (supposedly) in public, the postironic meme I tweet to my friends—I am indeed privatizing my care for language. I am embracing a not-in-my-backyard approach to language that reproduces generations' worth of redlining, covenants, suburban anxiety, racialized codes of appropriateness, and dubious logics about "safe space." I am using my and my intimates' idiolects as talismans against unforeseen incursions by others' equally beloved, equally talismanic, equally sense-making idiolects. And so, we cannot care only for the language we like. And yet we cannot honestly like the language that seems designed, focus-grouped, and fact-impervious enough to keep the majority of the world's populations quietly under its thumb. So it is perhaps the case that jumping into this business of caring for language cold is not the right approach. Maybe it's a simpler cognitive moment that is called for.

Make a Decision to Care for Language

If we decide to be willing to care for language, that means we don't quite need to know how to do it yet. We don't have to be experts or even particularly adept at knowing which language to care for in a given moment and in a given way. Simply, we decide that language is worth *our* caring about. This step is in fact much more profound than it seems, given how many imperatives there are in our environments telling us to ignore, weaponize, fear, scrub down, reformat, or monetize language—but never to care of it. In making this decision, we can take inspiration from Deborah Tannen's early work in her germinal 1981 essay on New York Jewish Conversational Style, where she wrote that: "The emotional/aesthetic experience of a perfectly tuned conversation is as ecstatic as an artistic experience. The satisfaction of having communicated successfully goes beyond the pleasure of being understood in the narrow sense. It is a ratification of one's place in the world and one's way of being human. It is, as Becker calls a well-performed shadowplay, a 'vision of sanity'" (1978, p. 145; note that Tannen derives this conception of "a vision of sanity" from the American linguist Alton Becker's essay on Javanese theater, 1979).

If we are unsure in dark times whose and what language is worthy of caring for, and we tend to want to fortify our own community languages as a way to maintain dignity or sanity, perhaps Tannen's observation here can act as a kind of promissory note. Making a decision to care for language not only opens up the possibility to, as Annie Dillard says, "be in the market for some present tense" (1974, p. 85) around civic language use— to be on the lookout for language that ratifies new ways of being in the world, being human, being recognized, being sentient, being sane, being meaningful, or being dignified. It can also help us come to grips with the fact that others, who speak very differently than we may do, are often also experiencing the same caliber of delight in "perfectly tuned conversations" that appear to us shockingly out of tune, toneless, or indifferent to style. This is a phenomenon that Tannen refers to as the "opacity of style":

> To those unfamiliar with the workings of particular stylistic strategies, their use seems like evidence of lack of communication—which is simply to say they don't see how they work. More often than not the features used have

meaning in the speech habits of the different group, so conclusions are drawn based on what the signals would mean if the hearer had used them. [...] Style is often invisible. [...] People tend to take their conversational habits as self-evident and draw conclusions not about others' linguistic devices but about their intentions or personalities. (p. 144)

Making a decision to care about language means accepting responsibility for the inevitable and constant opacity of style, for the likelihood that others' language is necessarily going to be inscrutable enough to me to present serious barriers to my care for it. Hannah Arendt gestured toward something akin to the "opacity of style" in the immediate wake of the Shoah, in which more than half of European Jewry were murdered or driven out. In her 1947 essay "The Concentration Camps," Arendt argues that a kind of stylistic misalignment explained why postwar US readers were having such a hard time coming to grips with the truth of industrial mass murder under the Nazis. The stories that survivors told about their survival were simply too stylistically foreign to American readers' sensibilities around grief and suffering. Arendt announced that "There are numerous [...] reports by survivors; only a few have been published, partly because, quite understandably, the world wants to hear no more of these things, but also because they all leave the reader cold, that is, as apathetic and baffled as the writer himself, and fail to inspire those passions of outrage and sympathy through which men have always been mobilized for justice, for"—and here Arendt quotes the French Auschwitz survivor David Rousset—"misery that goes too deep arouses not compassion but repugnance" (1948, p. 743).

Making a decision to care for language would mean doing so in the case, and in the moment, of precisely such languages/idioms as Rousset and Arendt urgently speak about—language that is opaque to our immediately available intuitions of attunement. We must make a decision to presume in those opaque utterances a possible vision of sanity that is as crucial and central to their makers as in those that come most naturally to us, in our own favored forms of conversation and sense-making. This is a different commitment than, say, "being a good listener" or "showing empathy," because—among other things—language itself is here the primary beneficiary of our attention, rather than one person's direct experience. Perhaps counterintuitively, it is the attention to the specificity of language that makes further and ongoing attention to experience possible. As Hannah Arendt foresaw, demanding that language first be inspiring and brave *before* we care for it is a dangerous form of linguistic obedience, credulity, and injustice—the privilege of which we can no longer afford.

...As It Is Used

When he arrived in Paris, the French sociologist and student of language Pierre Bourdieu was a barrel-chested, countrified outsider with a strong Béarnese dialect and accent. His bodily and linguistic "habitus" did not fit well in Paris's refined intellectual institutions, and he had a hard time being taken seriously, listened to, and recognized as a thinker. Among Parisian insiders, there was much to joke about in Bourdieu's burly gait and earthy aspect. Over the decades, Bourdieu came to recognize this nudge-nudge wink-wink approach to linguistic discrimination as the workings of "symbolic power," which he wrote about under the aegis of "The Production and Reproduction of Legitimate Language" (1991). Symbolic power was a species of capital intricately invested in some persons and structurally withheld from others—by procedures of distinction in clothing, manner, disposition, speech, and indeed race, ethnicity, class, and gender. For Bourdieu, then, the orthodox notion that legitimate language was a right, an opportunity, and a potential achievement of all speakers was based on what he called the "illusion of linguistic communism that haunts all linguistic theory" (1991, p. 43). A French scholar, Bourdieu's notion of "linguistic theory" in this quotation did not mean "theory produced by professional linguists," but rather the sum total of ideas and discourses about language in civil society.

In Bourdieu's experience, the myth of French society was propelled forth by the conceit that everyone—even a burly Béarnaise newcomer—could speak like a Parisian if he wanted to, and this myth caused him a complex form of social suffering. Like US American classism, "the illusion of linguistic communism" runs on the idea that if people just tried harder, worked more, had the right teachers, seized the right opportunities, and cultivated the right desire, they (too!) could become (linguistically) rich. The illusion of linguistic communism and opportunity ensures then, ironically, that those whose language is registered as illegitimate—too loud, too inarticulate, too effusive, too accented, too variant, too lacking in rationality or critical affect—are themselves to blame for remaining illegitimate persons, precisely because their deficiency in language is regarded, in the end, as a voluntary form of recidivism.

Twenty years later, others would note that the power of linguistic discrimination had proliferated in civic society, as outward tolerance toward explicitly racist, sexist, and nativist judgments had become somewhat more muted in institutional settings (Cameron 1995). The communication studies scholar Deborah Cameron showed in *Verbal Hygiene* (1995) that the professions of linguistics and applied linguistics had long ago abandoned the effort to shape or criticize others' language use. This stance was rather taken up by columnists, political commentators, and cultural critics who tended to identify in this or that linguistic failing—notably, in spelling mistakes on home-made political placards or church marquees—the index of civil society's downfall. Without ado, these commentators would admonish education systems, teachers, religious organizations, absentee parents, and policy-makers as the cause of their society's apparent linguistic waywardness.

What Cameron and Bourdieu's work shows is that there is already a great deal of pressure on people to speak legitimately and correctly, and that caring for language ought perhaps to take a radically different path. What if, in "starting at the verbal end," we made a decision to care for the language that human beings actually make, rather than that which they *might* have made under some scenario of linguistic communism? Why not learn from theorists of bilingual education that a "deficit model" of language use only generates shame, anger, and reactionary resentment? A decision to care for language can be committed to caring for the language that is actually produced by persons, legitimately or illegitimately—persons whose linguistic habits and habitus are unlikely to change in the course of their lifetimes to fit the needs of any particular stylistic program or critical agenda. Perhaps we might place the focus of our care not on the preservation or production of hallowed new qualities of language, but on a predisposition to care for the language that we indeed tend to encounter, in interactions with others—whether in service encounters, call-center calls, student papers, sales pitches, mandatory employee greetings in chain coffee shops, holiday missives from family members, and elsewhere. These may not be our own preferred private idioms, nor our vision for civic interaction generally, but our thinly veiled disappointment in them does little to improve the daily quantum of "care for language" around us.

Among other things, Conversation Analysis and sociolinguistics provide us with a wide range of tools designed to help us to see, in detail and more precisely, how human beings do and do not speak, and how vastly idealized our abstract conceptions of human speech (ours and others' alike) tend to be. Gail Jefferson, one of the originators of Conversation Analysis in the 1970s, developed an intricate transcription system for face-to-face conversations that helped generations of researchers to devote care and attention to the ritual, interactional, and paralinguistic features of actual human talk in context (1983, 2004). And yet the potential applied benefit of CA—for health care, law, international relations, the therapeutic professions, poetics, and the creative arts—has hardly been imagined beyond its own specialist venues.

…As It Is Used in Interaction

Is not all language—even the driest, most disinterested, most inhumane-feeling language—intended, at some anthropological level, for interaction? In order to be conceived, strung together, stylized, and dispatched, all language (whether written, spoken, or silenced) has had, at some stage, to envision another who listens or is affected by it. Sometimes this "other," in the less-than-conscious awareness of the language-maker of the moment, is a vague composite of tens, hundreds, or thousands of other moments of interaction with real persons. At other times, language is made with a precise, if not accurate, apprehension of the intended recipient—who is also, always, an active and dynamic participant in the interaction, whether or not that recipient is directly present in the face-to-face context. Early twentieth-century linguistics gave us, however, a thoroughly and almost deliberately inadequate image of what linguistic interaction looks like. As the Latin Americanist Mary Louise Pratt (2012) points out, the influential Swiss linguist Ferdinand de Saussure's image of the "circuit of speech" has little to do with how human symbolic interaction actually takes place. Saussure's model of language-in-interaction pictures two genderless, ethnicity-less, race-less, skinless, bodiless heads, of equal status and rank, trading utterances without any apparent obstacles or difficulties. Of course, no such human exchange has ever taken place. Critiquing this canonical image, Pratt offers a counter-image from the seventeenth-century Andean political operative Felipe Guaman Poma de Ayala's visual rendering of an indigenous Quechua woman in linguistic interaction with a Spanish colonial priest, who intends to receive her confession. This lush, kinetic, and indeed fearful illustration of interaction returns to language the historical and material contexts proper to it, acknowledging that no human linguistic interaction has ever been ideal or free from the workings of power.

Heeding Pratt's (and Guaman Poma's) corrective teachings on the deficits of the Saussurean model, we can become committed to a perspective on interaction that is as unorthodox and disobedient as must be our perspective on language use. We cannot afford to build prescriptive, authoritative models for the care of language and linguistic interaction that are based on ideal virtues that represent the concerns of specific dominant cultures and classes—like transparency, security, non-interruption, calmness, clarity, thoroughness nor, heaven forbid, common ground. Though we may choose to cultivate these in our own individual speech repertoires, they do not make for inclusive guides in models of civic language. In her important book *Conflict Is Not Abuse*, the veteran queer feminist AIDS activist and novelist Sarah Schulman reminds us that, during the height of the US AIDS crisis in the 1980s, "Millions suffered and died without care, comfort, or interest, vilified by cruel projections, neglect, and unjustified exclusion and blame. [...] Only when people with AIDS and their friends intervened against the status quo and forced an end to the shunning by forcing interactivity through zaps, sit-ins, initiated agendas, actions, interruptions, shut-downs, exposes, research, and demonstrations, did systematic progress begin to be made" (2017). Schulman's crucial reminder here is that what constitutes ideal interaction depends on broader political and social conditions. If one's survival depends on interaction that others might find offensive and less than ideal, then those bystanders' models of interaction may be too narrow to care for language in its expansive civic entirety.

Indeed, the idea of "safe" language has also been shown in recent years to have a racist history. Christina Hanhardt's 2013 book *Safe Space: Gay Neighborhood History and the Politics of Violence* shows how the idea of and building of safe spaces has often resulted out of implicit and explicit attempts to exclude racialized low-income people and preempt interactions with them—in cities like New York, San Francisco, Berlin, and elsewhere. Jin Haritaworn's *Queer Lovers and Hateful Others* demonstrates similar dynamics in contemporary Germany's LGBT movements, which have routinely developed their conceptions of safe (interactional) space and language around the exclusion of Germany's young Muslim and Arab men. Hanhardt and Haritaworn's detailed studies show us a number of datasets and rationales about why civic linguistic interaction, in order to be just and real, must not be framed around prerequisite ground rules for decorum. Already in 1980, Tannen had demonstrated that there can be no general consensus, for instance, about whether interruption in conversation is a signal of disrespect and disinterest or, rather, of appreciation and involvement, "To those who do not expect overlap and interruption to be used cooperatively in conversation, and would not use it in that way themselves, another's overlap will be interpreted as a lack of attention" (1981, p. 144).

If we are unable to intuitively grasp the situated meaning of an interactional resource—like interrupting, gestures, jokes, or banter—we are likely to devalue it and rule it out of order. Consider the controversial case of the inscription (since removed) on Lei Yixin's mammoth "Stone of Hope" monument, memorializing the Reverend Dr. Martin Luther King, Jr. The poet Maya Angelou called for the removal of the inscription—which read "I was a drum major for justice, peace and righteousness"—because, in Angelou's words, this paraphrase of King's words make him "look like an arrogant twit. [...] He had a humility that comes from deep inside. The 'if' clause that is left out is salient. Leaving it out changes the meaning completely" (Weingarten and Ruane 2011). The missing if-clause, which for Angelou makes all the difference, comes from the full transcript of King's 1968 sermon at Atlanta's Ebenezer Baptist Church: "If you want to say that I was a drum major, say that I was a drum major for justice. Say that I was a drum major for peace. I was a drum major for righteousness. And all of the other shallow things will not matter" (King n.d.).

Angelou's intervention is certainly righteous on its own merit. But, in correcting the linguistic record, it leaves the *interactional* context of the sermon unaddressed. Those who participated in it attest, and audio recordings demonstrate, that King's "drum major" sermon is, as befitting the interactional genre of a Baptist sermon, interrupted by affirmative responses throughout by the congregation. It would have been utterly strange, in this genre's context, if worshippers had *not,* in the midst of the Reverend's sermon, called out "Make it plain! Make it plain!" and "What've we got here?" When a baby cries out during King's sermon, he responds immediately *to that baby*—without diverging from the flow of his sermon— by saying "Our first cry as a baby was a bid for attention." Though it is certainly conceivable that the builders of the Washington memorial to King might have included the entirety of King's utterance, including its if-clause, it is difficult to imagine a kind of traditional, permanent public monument that would be able to express care for the interactional elements of this speech situation. This is a problem of the divide, and discrepancy of value, between literate documentary culture and oral interactional culture, one which makes care for language particularly elusive. One major component of linguistic disobedience then is always to imagine the primary nature of interactional context to language itself, to imagine what it would mean to care for, recognize, and indeed memorialize the singular virtuosity—or the singular catastrophe—of language events.

...As It Is Used in Human Interaction

It may be important to further propose that there is something specific about caring for language in *human* interaction, lest we imagine that linguistic interaction *without* humans' involvement would be just about the same as linguistic interaction *between* them are. Consider the 2016 film

Arrival (dir. Dennis Villeneuve) which, far more than other recent mainstream explorations of communicating with extraterrestrial nonhuman aliens (like *Battlestar Galactica*), attempted to characterize linguistic interaction between a human professional linguist, Louise Banks, and her extraterrestrial interlocutors as an encounter with radical difference. The plot of the film focused on Banks' genial attempts to decode the nature of the extraterrestrials' linguistic system and orthography, and her expertise in this realm was demonstrated by way of her ability to distill the mathematical regularity of the signs they produced. The film, in rendering extraterrestrial languages readable by human (mathematical) means, seems to undermine everything that makes human language so puzzlingly human.

What's further puzzling though is how conventionally human the *interactions* between human and extraterrestrial in the film turned out to be. Separated by an opaque screen, the human and extraterrestrial communicators in *Arrival* interacted with one another in extraordinarily regular human-species-defining ways. Forty years of research in Conversation Analysis, sociology of language, and conversational pragmatics—as well as the anthropology of ritual before them—have given us a wide range of concepts and principles through which to apprehend the stunning regularity and anthropological conventionality of human conversation, when it is utterly possible to imagine communication taking place in radically different ways for such hypothetical beings as those pictured in *Arrival*. The interacting parties in the film, to take a few simple features, observe without fail the *human* regularity of orderly conversational turn-taking (Sacks et al. 1974) as well as those of H. Paul Grice's Cooperative Principle (1975), providing the kind of responses that satisfy human expectational horizons of appropriate relevance, expressive manner, evidentiary quality, and informational quantity—features particular to human face-to-face interaction—even if the extraterrestrials appear to be speaking a radically different *langue*. So, not only does *Arrival* anthropomorphize the aliens' language *systems*, to whatever extent such a systematicity can even be ascribed, the film characterizes the interactional norms of the extraterrestrials as essentially identical to those found among humans: taking turns, facing one another, giving face, repairing threats to face, and so on.

Why does this matter for how we think about caring for language? Since Erving Goffman, social science researchers have insisted that humans have developed and become stunningly competent at a range of peculiarly effective species-level "interactional resources" that cannot be attributed to humans' inherent linguistic *faculty* alone—resources that have become such an intuitive substrate of our various cultures that we hardly notice them. These extraordinary and extraordinarily social human competences belong to shy, quiet, introverted, and awkward folks as much as they do to those traditionally pegged as conversation savvy "people people." (On the notion of a "narrow" linguistic faculty that distinguishes humans from other communicating animals, see Hauser et al. 2002.) Our more or less innate faculty to generate complex recursive syntax cannot explain the intersubjective and interactional capacities and intuitions that humans universally engage in. Malinowski (1923) suggested, for instance, the universality of what he called "phatic communion"—that is, "free, aimless, social intercourse [in which...] the meaning of its words is almost completely irrelevant" (297). For Malinowski, this kind of contact communion through language—between friends, lovers, strangers, and enemies alike—demonstrates "the fundamental tendency which makes the mere presence of others a necessity for man [sic]" (297) and therefore highlights small-talk and other apparently intellectually unchallenging forms of talk as "one of the bedrock aspects of man's nature in society" (296).

Malinowski thus did much to return language to its proper interactional situation between humans, after it had long been held hostage by zealously scientistic Young Grammarians like Hermann Osthoff and Karl Brugmann. But this nineteenth-century vision of language as primarily a morphological puzzle, rather than an interactional one, continued to hold sway deep into the late twentieth century. This paradigmatic imbalance made it difficult, beginning in the 1970s for instance, to talk critically about things like sexist and racist language, because these were assumed to be either (1) lexico-grammatical properties of language itself or (2) psychosocial properties of language users themselves. What went almost entirely missing from the equation was language *in interaction*. Lay and expert analysts alike had a grim choice between pinning racism, sexism, homophobia, elitism, classism, colonialism, and so on, on persons (who use language) or on language (as used by persons). This led, in part, to the shrill and reactionary culture of white victimhood, in which persons who had historically enjoyed the ability to dilate in hegemonic language suddenly found themselves the object of characterological and linguistic critique. Having enjoyed hegemonic status thus far, these advantage-seekers did what was rational to them: they sought to retain hegemonic prerogative in language—through violence, cunning, brute force, disfiguration, and the symbolic resources at their disposal. Very little public discourse in the 1990s United States, for instance, was dedicated to monitoring the maneuvers by which powerful reactionaries were discovering language—as a new frontier for consolidating their structural advantage in our societies and institutions. Meanwhile, many of us everyday users of language tended to deny or minimize our own spectacular linguistic competencies, convinced as we were that the gift of being good at, or at ease in, language belonged to an ambitious elite of talkers, networkers, influencers, and wave-makers.

Had Western/Global Northern societies benefitted much earlier—say in the seventeenth to nineteenth centuries—from a science of human linguistic *interaction* rather than of linguistic *systems* alone, we would not have had to wait so long for insights from such twenty-first century researchers like the anthropologist Jane Hill (1993) and sociolinguist Scott Kiesling. Kiesling, for instance, in a 2001 study on "Stances of Whiteness and Hegemony in Fraternity Men's Discourse" develops an understanding of the ways young white-identified men at a university fraternity intuitively though unwittingly cultivate white privilege in conversation, even without resorting to overt anti-Black racist talk. These young men were angling not so much for racial privilege as such, for but *interactional* privilege more generally, by which Kiesling means a range of coded meta-strategies to keep the upper-hand in a conversational setting. This dispositional pursuit of the interactional upper-hand doesn't mean conspicuous power plays and dominance, as much as evoking certain discourses of freedom and favorability—through attributes like certainty, rationality, impartiality, and easy-goingness. The young men, so Kiesling shows, deploy these interactional resources so as to maintain hegemonic sway over what gets talked about and how, what range of cultural references can be made, which tones can be used, and which epistemic and affective stances are regarded as comprehensible. Kiesling explains how this stance-taking often involves appropriating Black vernaculars, when the purposes of interactional advantage justify it:

In the metastrategy of race-modeled stance taking, the mostly White-identified men use Black linguistic styles in order to take stances stereotypically indexed to Black masculinity, in speech domains characteristically associated with Black culture. While this linguistic appropriation would seem to indicate an acknowledgment of some kind of Black prestige, it in fact only works interactionally because of the unequal power relationships of Black and White. (101)

What Kiesling's analysis shows us is that a critique of language itself, or a critique of language users' ideologies, does not leave enough room for understanding the relationship between interactional resources and social structures. These young white-identified men are not engaging in speech traditionally thought to be racist itself, but their habitual, hegemonic forms of talk are reliably able of carrying out racist effects. This means that the long-held "3I" paradigm of language (language as an Internal, Individual, and Inherent faculty, Steffensen 2015), which has guided most insight about hate speech and freedom of speech throughout the twentieth century, is blind to those realms of human linguistic interaction that are equally in need of our care. Bringing the tools of Conversation Analysis, pragmatics, and sociolinguistics into everyday discussions of linguistic justice is thus a promising, belated corrective.

...As It Is Used in Human and Nonhuman Interaction

But languages can interact with one another these days without human involvement. A quick survey of the Web site and research output of the Institute of Electrical and Electronic Engineers (IEEE.org) shows its affiliates to be hard at work on the problem of how languages interact with other languages on automatic, algorithmically managed platforms. Certainly there is a human being somewhere in the mix, but her or his involvement is analogous to an announcer at a hockey game, rather than a player, or the puck in play. In this age of language "use," cross-linguistic data management and machine translation—in matters as diverse as petroleum extraction, securitarian architecture, global credit-debit relations, immigration-control technology, and other means of production—have unhinged themselves from any individual hegemonic language (say,

English) and begin to administer global systems. Translationally mediated and fortified concepts, styles, and control repertoires are developed, which in turn distribute procedures, protocols, and norms globally, with varying degrees of success. These varying degrees of success are the wheelhouse and promise of computational engineers, who ceaselessly innovate ways to close the gaps of optimization, translatability, and logistical supply-chain management. This process of innovation requires the continual discovery of words, concepts, and styles as a uniquely promising site for industrial prospecting, securitization, and financialization in late capitalism.

Such technologically innovated and exponential global coordination has required the development of a translatability industry since 1990 to ensure the easy transfer of meaning across language frontiers in the normal course of industrial exchange, global credit-debit relations, and cybertraffic. Ours is an age in which the effects of ecologically destructive language and discourse are amplified and multiplied, to the extent that, for instance, petroleum-extractive industries must be able to produce and induce their specific meanings in scores of commercial languages simultaneously. Thus the task of caring for language is now more than ever involved in high-stakes endeavors to reimagine an ecologically habitable "green grammar" (Goatly 1996), and to discern the planet-sustaining or -destroying "stories we live by" (Stibbe 2015).

…In Complex, Multilayered Ways

The applied linguist Li Wei has suggested that the principle of caring for language must be unhinged from deeply held monolingualist habits around what constitutes good language use, behavior, and practice. Those users of language who have developed for themselves a "translanguaging instinct" (Li Wei 2017)—that is, those who "use [their] idiolect or linguistic repertoire without regard for socially and politically defined language labels or boundaries—in order to make sense, solve problems, articulate one's thought, and gain knowledge" (16)—are often dismissed in language policy debates, educational curricular design, literary theory, and powerfully conventional conceptions of linguistic identity, articulacy and competence. So much for linguistic communism. As Michael Billig suggests, it is a particularly modern requirement that humans—in order to enter into normal daily communication—must be registered as speaking a particular language "object," like English, German, or Igbo (1995, p. 31). Translanguagers, code-meshers, and other conveyers of mixed language throw a wrench into this tightly monitored set of socio-institutional expectations, forming a particular flank in the planetary endeavor of linguistic disobedience.

In this scheme of things, "multilingualism" is not always on the side of the angels. Global Northern/Western conceptions of multilingualism as a pluralization of orderly monolingualisms often end up promoting reactionary, securitarian, or neoliberal agendas. Robert Moore, in his 2015 essay on "reactionary multilingualism," compares the contemporary European Commission's policy on universal civic trilingualism to Revolutionary France's endeavors to ideologically unify mainland France through monolingualism. In both scenarios, "the spectre of miscommunication—caused perhaps by speakers with less-than-perfect fluency in a/ the Standard, and/or through their use of an inherently flawed verbal instrument—is viewed with undisguised horror, and is seen as a threat to governance and social cohesion" (Moore 2015, p. 20). (Notably, the educational linguist Moore penned this analysis prior to Brexit and the 2016 US election cycle.) The rise and rebranding (Katznelson and Bernstein 2017) of reactionary multilingualism means that caring for language cannot merely mean 'promoting language learning' or 'increasing the amount of languages spoken.' Care for language in a complex political entity like the European Union might take the shape, rather, of gaining a better understanding of the language- and meaning-based repertoires that are actually spoken and made useful in European territory, parsing out what functions they serve for those who use them, and explaining how these repertoires meaningfully diverge from the dominant monolingual model.

...In Times of Great Need, and Spaces of Great Suffering

"The anger window is open," wrote Rebecca Traister in November 2017 about powerful white men's serial sexual predation of women working for them in politics, the entertainment industry, and academia.

Women's accounts of having quietly or not-so-quietly tolerated abuse, gaslighting, and entrapment by men in workplace settings surged into public discussion, while a sitting President of the United States seemed to easily glide above, despite 16 named accusers. If they'd forgotten, people remembered what they and each other had said or not said 26 years prior about Anita Hill, "a woman with unusual insight into this topic" as Jane Mayer of *The New Yorker* put it (2017). A generation of young liberal-minded straight white cisgender men on university campuses caught a glimpse for the first time in November 2017 of what it might feel like to be interactionally constrained by symbolic relations of power, to be nonhegemonic in their daily conversational exchanges. Young women told their teachers, regardless of the scheduled topics of their classes, that they wanted to talk about sexual assault and how to stop it. The anger window was open.

What does it mean for an anger window to be open? For three years prior to 2017, organized, creative, and loud Black Lives Matter undertakings had publicly envisioned counterworlds of justice, language, and morality that seemed to have no place in the institutions they were calling to account (Mackin 2016). Occupy Wall Street and Gezi Park had been immoderate, urgent expressions of divestment from statist paternalism and the "cruel optimism" of neoliberal master-narratives (Berlant 2011). Traister's pronouncement was not about the nature and imminence of human anger—which has ever been, and has ever been ignorable by the powerful—but rather about the infrastructure of American civic communication since 2017. Something opened that cannot be closed. The bad deals (of patriarchy, white/settler supremacy, hetero/homonormativity, nativism and plutocracy)—deals that had always been so riddled with rotten deal-breakers that they were hard to count—were called to a general public audit. And yet, the President was saying atrocious, racist, misogynist things over and over and over. The anger window was open. Was it still even a window? What language had its frame been made of?

...Whether This Language Is an Act of Labor, Work, Leisure, or Pleasure

Is there a reliable boundary between what we say at work and what we say at leisure—and the styles and repertoires of our doing so? In her essay on queer value, Meg Wesling suggested that psychic and cultural meaning-making practices (desires, utterances, performances, art, even ideation) cannot be thought of as a protected, pre-economic domain, protected from the coercions of capitalism. Even our most idiolectal, eccentric, antinormative, and disobedient formulations are implicated— not merely because they take place under conditions of political hegemony and neocolonialism for instance, but because they can easily become "compulsory gendered labor that accrues value for capitalism without monetary remuneration for the individual laborer" (109). Even when we may think our language, for instance, is private, wayward, or noncompliant with neoliberal orders of competition and interaction, it may turn out to be precisely a form of labor, in the Arendtian sense that "it is indeed the mark of all laboring that it leaves nothing behind, that the result of its effort is almost as quickly consumed as the effort is spent" (Arendt 1958, p. 58).

We often cannot tell when a person is speaking as a form of work, labor, leisure, pleasure, or something else entirely. As with the prudence of critique and correction, it is important not to reject or withhold care for language simply because we believe, in a given moment, that it is being used for commercial purposes only. We must remain at least provisionally agnostic when tempted to identify a particular motivation behind a string of talk in which we are involved. No one, including the speaker, knows entirely what motivates the creative, volatile, and ambiguous activity we call speaking in any given moment.

But the poem of language care is still only beginning. We are told to "begin at the verbal end," but this is of course just a beginning, an axiom, a guide for engagement. Most powerful political leaders since 1990 have become masters of linguistic and moral relativism and have indeed accrued much of their power by turning this relativism into an interactional weapon. Thanks to predator-pollsters and focus-groupers like Frank Luntz, high-profile and/or behind-the-scenes power-brokers (who may not be particularly dextrous around language on their own) have nonetheless been schooled in how and why to manipulate language for their immediate needs. Changing one word in a campaign platform can easily mean winning an election, beating a popular referendum, or undermining a rising star from an opposition party. While the 1960s and 1970s housed great discoveries around language and culture, the 1980s was the first age in which sensibilities around the cultural politics of linguistic relativism were industrialized, institutionalized, and militarized. Currently powerful despots and demagogues have profited from this revolution in language, not because they are particularly astute or careful about language themselves, but because they have the funds to hire armies of consultants and message-makers to manage their language for them.

But the point of our suggestions about "caring for language" is not to focus on language itself as an autonomous or relativistic hall-of-mirrors for play, slippage, possibility, or advantage. That's what the worst of our leaders are already doing. We need to end our poem with a suggestion that makes all of this care worth it—in the world, in this moment, and amid the constraints with which we and our fellows live. To this end, we will simply add the following additional line:

> Make a decision
> to care for language
> as it is used
> in human and nonhuman interaction
> in complex, multilayered ways
> in times of great need
> and spaces of great suffering
> whether this language
> is an act of labor, work,
> leisure, pleasure,
> Or something else.
> **Care for this language**
> **Always in its recursive relation**
> **To reality.**

No further qualification is necessary, we think. The "relation to reality" we add as a fundamental component of caring for language does not mean to suggest that language is divorced from reality, that it is not part of reality, or that it by nature undermines reality. But we are aware that there are symbolic systems (numerical, cosmological, sensory, embodied, nutritional, agricultural, spiritual, and stratigraphic) that, though they are in relation to language, are not reducible to it. Numerical data, water temperatures, sea-level rise, toxicity rates, complex processes of physics and the like: all of these heralds of reality are what make caring for language so utterly crucial. So, too, do cosmologies: spiritual, theological, ethical, humanist, futurist, deconstructionist stances of knowledge and commitment are the ground—sometimes indeed the groundless ground—upon which we know how and why to make language matter, to care for language. But why "recursive"? Why isn't "relation to reality" good enough? It was a German Romantic poet who sought to show in his work "daß die Worte sich selbst oft besser verstehen, als diejenigen von denen sie gebraucht werden" ("that words often understand one another better than those by whom they are used" Schlegel 1967, p. 364, translation by Christian Steinmetz). Amid the active use of words, we are unable to constantly analyze their immediate relation to reality. Words tend to be more responsible to the words that have come before them and to those that are to come, in the flow of a given utterance, than they are to the discrete objects I may appear to be referring to while speaking. Try as I might to be precise, appropriate, and accurate, there is always something uncontrolled and uncontrollable about language-in-use, something that seventeenth-century linguists desperately wanted to contain precisely and that twenty-first-century call-center-employee-handbook writers have sought to regulate precisely.

Caring for language is not about slowing language down or bidding of it that it be something other than what it is—sometimes spastic, sometimes lugubrious, sometimes spontaneously revelatory, sometimes utterly numbing. Caring for language always in its recursive relation to reality means that we intend, at regular daily intervals, to return to and face the evidentiary world, as we can best understand it.

Consider the sense of unmoored, festive dizziness that was at the heart of the supposedly structuralist Ferdinand de Saussure's theoretical endeavor about language all along—especially in his late work, where he develops the following metaphor: "A sign system must be part of a community. Indeed, any semiological system is not a ship in dry dock, but a ship in the open sea. Which is the real ship: one in the covered yard surrounded by engineers, or a ship at sea? Quite clearly only a ship at sea may yield information about the nature of a ship. A community environment changes everything. A sign system is destined for a community just as a ship is destined for the sea" (cited in Holquist 2014, p. 13). Following Saussure's metaphor, the recursive relation to reality for which we care is decidedly not the habitual impulse to desire quiet seas, to make it back to land, or even to purchase better navigation instruments. It is in fact the opposite of these things: the realization that the movement, volatility, and excitement of being at sea is an expression of the complex reality of our positions in the world at any given moment. Wishing to return to land, to be in "dry dock," as Saussure says, may be caring for something—for an imagined homeland, for relations that used to make better sense to us, for traditions that felt solid and honorable, but such homesickness for scientific (mono)lingualism is destined to efface the living world around us. Our communities, our meanings, and our futures are out at sea.

References

Appadurai, Arjun. *Banking on Words: The Failure of Language in the Age of Derivative Finance*. Chicago: University of Chicago Press, 2016.

Arendt, Hannah. "The Concentration Camps." *Partisan Review* 15, no. 7 (1948): 743–763.

Arendt, Hannah. *The Human Condition*. Chicago: University of Chicago Press, 1958.

Becker, Alton. "Text-Building, Epistemology and Aesthetics in Javanese Shadow Theatre." In *The Imagination of Reality: Essays in Southeast Asian Coherence Systems*, edited by A. L. Becker and A. A. Yengoyan. Norwood, NJ: Ablex, 1978.

Berlant, Lauren. *Cruel Optimism*. Durham, NC: Duke University Press, 2011.

Billig, Michael. *Banal Nationalism*. London: Sage Publications, 1995.

Blanchet, Philippe. *Discriminations: combattre la glottophobie*. Paris: Textuel, 2016.

Bourdieu, Pierre. *Language and Symbolic Power*, edited and translated by John B. Thompson. Cambridge: Polity Press, 1991.

Bourdieu, Pierre. *Distinction: A Social Critique of the Judgement of Taste*. Translated by Richard Nice. Cambridge, MA: Harvard University Press, 2015.

Chandler McEntyre, Marilyn. *Caring for Words in a Culture of Lies*. Grand Rapids, MI: Eerdmans, 2009.

Cameron, Deborah. *Verbal Hygiene*. London: Routledge, 1995.

Cameron, Deborah. *Good to Talk? Living and Working in a Communication Culture*. New York: Sage, 2000.

Cameron, Deborah. "Language from the Top Down." *Language and Communication* 28 (2008): 143–155.

Canagarajah, A. Suresh. "Codemeshing in Academic Writing: Identifying Teachable Strategies of Translanguaging." *Modern Language Journal* 95, no. 3 (2011): 401–417.

Clifton, Lucille. *The Collected Poems of Lucille Clifton*. New York: BOA Editions Ltd., 2015.

Dillard, Annie. *Pilgrim at Tinker Creek*. New York: Olive Editions, 2016.

Dembeck, Till. "Multilingual Philology and National Literature: Re-reading Classical Texts." *Critical Multilingualism Studies* 5, no. 3 (2017): 2–12.

Duchêne, Alexandre and Monica Heller. *Language in Late Capitalism: Pride and Profit*. London: Routledge, 2012.

Flores, Nelson and Jonathan Rosa. "Undoing Appropriateness: Raciolinguistic Ideologies and Language Diversity in Education." *Harvard Educational Review* 85, no. 2 (2015): 149–172.

Gaeta, Luciano. "Così ho rivissuto *Il processo* di Kafka." *La Stampa* [Torino], April 9, 1983.

Hanhardt, Christina. *Safe Space: Gay Neighborhood History and the Politics of Violence*. Durham: Duke University Press, 2013.

Hauser, Marc, Noam Chomsky, and Tecumseh Fitch. "The Faculty of Language: What Is It, Who Has It, and How Did It Evolve?" *Science* 298, no. 5598 (2002): 1569–1579.

Herder, Johann Gottfried. "Über die neuere deutsche Literatur." In *Werke*, edited by Günter Arnold et al. 1: 161–649. Frankfurt am Main: Deutscher Klassiker Verlag, 1985–2000 [1767–1768].

Haritaworn, Jinthana. *Queer Lovers and Hateful Others: Regenerating Violent Times and Places.* London: Pluto Press, 2015.

Hill, Jane H. "Hasta La Vista, Baby: Anglo Spanish in the American Southwest." *Critique of Anthropology* 13, no. 2 (1993): 145–176.

Holquist, Michael. "What Would Bakhtin Do?" *Critical Multilingualism Studies* 2, no. 1 (2014): 6–19.

Gilligan, Carol. *In a Different Voice: Psychological Theory and Women's Development.* Cambridge, MA: Harvard University Press, 1982.

Goatly, Andrew. "Green Grammar and Grammatical Metaphor." *Journal of Pragmatics* 25 (1996): 537–560.

Grice, H. Paul. "Logic and Conversation." In *Syntax and Semantics. Vol 3, Speech Acts*, edited by Peter Cole and Jerry L. Morgan. 41–58. New York: Academic Press, 1975.

Jefferson, Gail. "Issues in the Transcription of Naturally-Occurring Talk: Caricature vs. Capturing Pronounciational Particulars." *Tilburg Papers in Language and Literature* 34 (1983).

Jefferson, Gail. "Glossary of Transcript Symbols with an Introduction." In *Conversation Analysis: Studies from the First Generation*, edited by Gene H. Lerner. 13–31. Amsterdam: John Benjamins, 2004.

Katznelson, Noah and Katie Bernstein. "Rebranding Bilingualism: The Shifting Discourses of Language Education Policy in California's 2016 Election." *Linguistics and Education* 40 (2017): 11–26.

King, Martin Luther. "The Drum Major Instinct." Recorded on 4 November 1968 at Ebenezer Baptist Church. Accessed December, 17, 2017. http://okra.stanford.edu/media/audio/680204000.mp3.

Kiesling, Scott. "Stances of Whiteness and Hegemony in Fraternity Men's Discourse." *Journal of Linguistic Anthropology* 11, no. 1 (2001): 101–115.

Lezra, Jacques. "This Untranslatability Which Is Not One." *Paragraph* 38, no. 2 (2015): 174–188.

Li Wei. "Translanguaging as a Practical Theory of Language." *Applied Linguistics* 39 (2017): 1–23.

Mackin, Glenn. "Black Lives Matter and the Concept of the Counterworld." *Philosophy and Rhetoric* 49, no. 4 (2016): 459–481.

Malinowski, Bronislaw. "The Problem of Meaning in Primitive Languages." In *The Meaning of Meaning*, edited by C. K Ogden and I. A. Richards. 296–336. London: Routledge & Kegan Paul, 1923.

Mayer, Jane. "Anita Hill on Weinstein, Trump, and a Watershed Moment for Sexual-Harassment Accusations." *The New Yorker*, November 1, 2017.

Moore, Robert. "From Revolutionary Monolingualism to Reactionary Multilingualism: Top-Down Discourses of Linguistic Diversity in Europe, 1794–Present." *Language and Communication* 44 (2015): 19–30.

Oard, Douglas. "Transcending the Tower of Babel: Supporting Access to Multilingual Information with Cross-Language Information Retrieval." In *Emergent Information Technologies and Enabling Policies for Counter-Terrorism*, edited by Robert Popp and John Yen. 299–314. IEEE Press Series on Computational Intelligence, 2006.

Phipps, Alison. "Language Plenty, Refugees, and the Post-Brexit World: New Practices from Scotland." In *Languages After Brexit: How the UK Speaks to the World*, edited by M. Kelly, 95–107. Cham, Switzerland: Palgrave Macmillan, 2017.

Pratt, Mary Louise. "The Traffic in Meaning: Translation, Contagion, Infiltration." *Profession* 2002 (2002): 25–36.

Pratt, Mary Louise. "If English Was Good Enough for Jesus: Monolinguismo y mala fe." *Critical Multilingualism Studies* 1, no. 1 (2012): 12–30.

Pym, Anthony. *The Moving Text: Localization, Translation and Distribution*. Philadelphia: John Benjamins, 2004.

Ricento, Thomas. "Historical and Theoretical Perspectives in Language Policy and Planning." *Journal of Sociolinguistics* 4, no. 2 (2000): 196–213.

Sacks, Harvey, Emanuel Schegloff and Gail Jefferson. "A Simplest Systematics for the Organization of Turn-Taking for Conversation." *Language* 50 (1974): 696–735.

Schlegel, Friedrich. "Über die Unverständlichkeit." In *Kritische Friedrich Schlegel Ausgabe* 2, edited by Hans Eichner. 363–372. Munich: Schöningh, 1967.

Schulman, Sarah. *The Mere Future*. Vancouver: Arsenal Pulp Press, 2011.

Schulman, Sarah. *Conflict Is Not Abuse: Overstating Harm, Community Responsibility, and the Duty of Repair*. Vancouver: Arsenal Pulp Press, 2017.

Steffensen, Sune Vork. "Distributed Language and Dialogism: Notes on Non-locality, Sense-Making and Interactivity." *Language Sciences* 50 (2015): 105–19.

Stibbe, Arran. *Ecolinguistics: Language, Ecology, and the Stories We Live by*. London: Routledge, 2015.

de Swaan, Abram. *Words of the World: The Global Language System*. Cambridge: Polity, 2001.

Tannen, Deborah. "New York Jewish Conversational Style." *International Journal of the Sociology of Language* 30 (1981): 133–149.

Thorne, Stephen. Plenary Address: "Technologies, Morphologies of Communicative Action, and the Rewilding of Language education." American Association for Applied Linguistics, Chicago, Illinois, March 25, 2018.

Traister, Rebecca. "Your Reckoning. And Mine. As Stories About Abuse, Assault, and Complicity Come Flooding Out, How Do We Think About the Culprits in Our Lives? Including, Sometimes, Ourselves." *The Cut*, November 12, 2017. https://www.thecut.com/2017/11/rebecca-traister-on-the-post-weinstein-reckoning.html.

Watson, Jean. *Nursing: The Philosophy and Science of Caring*. Little, Brown and Co., 1979.

Weingarten, Gene and Michael Ruane. "Maya Angelou Says King Memorial Inscription Makes Him Look 'Arrogant'." *The Washington Post*, August 30, 2011.

Wesling, Meg. "Queer Value." *GLQ: A Journal of Lesbian and Gay Studies* 18, no. 1 (2012): 107–125.

5

Epilogue: Finding Our Minds

Losing Our Minds

Changing our minds about how we understand, engage with, and use individual and shared language(s) is a straightforward decision in theory—less so in practice. Roadblocks litter the path. Even finding the capacity to concentrate amidst the rolling barrage of terrible news, falsehoods, and screen-tested invective feels like a major accomplishment. One day brings a ban on people entering our lives or reentering their own. The next morning announces a ban, or a war, on words we find essential to our and our fellows' livelihoods. Making the choice *what* to read, too, takes on new meaning, when things to read self-update on our phones and social media news feeds, more often than they arrive in our email inboxes and old-fashioned mailboxes—that is, when they bear less and less of what we might expect of actual worldly things: some kind of modest permanence, imprint, or evidentiary promise.

An unavoidable obstacle is the heavily mediated perception of our age as the age of shock events. Historian Heather C. Richardson championed this term in late January 2017, after Donald Trump's first executive order had temporarily barred nationals of seven predominantly Muslim countries from US entry. Shock events, despite the usual semantic contingency that we invoke on so many occasions, live up to their name quite exactly. They are

© The Author(s) 2019
Y. Komska et al., *Linguistic Disobedience*,
https://doi.org/10.1007/978-3-319-92010-8_5

unsolicited, unreviewed, unexpected, unprecedented. They take our breath away, they overwhelm, confuse, and exhaust. They entrench the time-tested imperial model of the all-pervasive "omnicrisis" (Hardt and Negri 2004, p. 36)—the perpetual state of emergency that, supposedly, only top-down interventions can resolve, despite their having provoked and sustained it— in what continues to be understood as a democratic society. Shock events put us, perceptibly, on the brink of losing our minds. That is, in fact, their purpose. And it is very hard to change a mind that feels lost.

The state propagates crises—real, imagined, and too crazy to be fiction. A crisis-managerial elite arises at the taxpayers' cost, though citizens themselves rarely get the resources to foster the kinds of civic competence that might help them navigate or avert crises. This is no new development. And yet, not all is lost: "once disaster strikes [...] ordinary citizens realize how important they are," writes journalist Amanda Ripley (2008, p. xiii). Being woke, an ideal of critical civic awareness popularized by the Black Lives Matter movement, remains an inspired yet rare illustration of how a word and a moral value from African-American Vernacular English has been able to pass meaningfully into mainstream usage in the 2010s, though its use quickly became controversial.

What everyday antidotes are there to shock events, gaslighting, denial, deflection, and everything else that renews the daily prospect of losing one's mind? What can help us regain our minds? How can we dismantle elite bastions of expertise without questioning the fundamental premises of being an expert—the command of evidence, judgment, expressive capacity, experience, and so on? Of course, there are critique, correction, and care, about which we write, but these take long-term commitment. This epilogue, in contrast to the rest of the book, focuses on "obeying" the minor jolts and minute awakenings of daily awareness, on foregrounding everyday experiences of disorientation that counteract the chaos around us, on relating the vulnerabilities that render us open and humble instead of shut-down and compliant, on deep immersion in the perceptual and interactional world. They are moments when we have been surprised by and confronted with some kind of language that has had the potency to bring us one step closer to meaningful linguistic disobedience—to refusing the spoils of interactional hegemony in our use of languages.

In these encounters, simply paying attention plays an important role. "Disengagement from a broader field of attraction [...] for the sake of isolating or focusing on a reduced number of stimuli," as attention has been defined, is not an innocent notion (Crary 1999, p. 1). Once considered a "local" exercise of personal choices in pursuit of self-presentation, etiquette, or learning (Crary 1999, p. 14), in capitalist modernity the social and scientific turn toward attention took the shape of an imposition upon individuals. Their patterns of labor, education, consumption, and even leisure were to be steered and optimized, with the goal of rendering subjects productive and manageable, "socially integrated and adaptive" (Crary 1999, p. 4). Yoked to the rules of industrial rationalization and regulation—be it on factory assembly lines or in marketing schemes for new inventions, from Thomas Alva Edison's Kinetoscope (a precursor to motion-picture projectors) to Steve Jobs' designs for Apple—paying attention has been substantially implicated in inculcating obedience or, at very least, in the attempts to inculcate it.

And yet, substantially does not mean entirely. The relentless pursuit of attention—and the fact that attention persists as a "problem," with solutions escaping present-day scientists, CEOs, marketing executives, and educational optimization gurus as much as they once evaded these professionals' nineteenth-century predecessors—suggests that humans routinely dodge the nets of "institutional capture" (Crary 1999, p. 3). They devise new rituals of inattention. They reinvent attention on their own terms: like language, paying attention was never a domain usurped by a single actor. Consider the formerly ISIS-occupied parts of Iraq, where the contemplation of art, music, or literature remained impervious to control even under the dire threat of death. Secretly, people wrote and recited poetry, they hummed the unforgotten melodies, they buried the books and instruments to protect these from purposeful destruction. Such moments of rapt attention become "an exemption from ordinary condition," a way to break with control, and a disobedient stance (Crary 1999, p. 10).

It is such moments that we would like to highlight, in conclusion. Panic and widespread despondency notwithstanding (or maybe due to them), these instances couldn't be timelier amid the new push for more independent forms of attention, for more sobriety. Leslie Jamison's recent writings on sobriety in the most literal sense, to name one example, do more than decry the cultural fixation on art produced in the state of intoxication—or on the "genius" artist-addict. They also steer clear of praising the largely unsung condition of sobriety, oft-dismissed for its apparent tedium and scant generative possibilities, as a source of self-beneficial wellness or "metabolized recovery." The ultimate prize of sobriety is not even creative "jet fuel," one learns (Jamison 2018). Instead, the true benefit of sober lucidity, per Jamison, is "paying attention to lives outside of your own," "engaging with other people's stories" (Shapiro 2018). Taken metaphorically, such sobriety echoes in this book's trajectory, proceeding as it does from a retreat into critique to considered engagement in correction to caring for the language of others. In finding our own minds, we discover the minds of others.

In the spirit of vulnerability, we have decided to share a very personal, unrepresentative archive of only three discoveries. We chose three because there are three of us, and not because there's anything magical about the number three. These recent encounters changed our own minds about language, made us temporarily "exempt" from relentless news-cycle noise, focused our attention on what matters. Their power lies in employing language as always visual, always imperceptibly violent, and always embodied or tactile. "Words can kill," of course, is a common turn of phrase proven true by neuroscientists who study the impact of long-term verbal stress (Teicher et al. 2010). We should not discount that. And yet, the ways in which language transports violence can be stubbornly generative, not just destructive. The resulting surprises and confrontations reawaken us to inescapable historical truths and, not least, to our own disobedient selves, asleep for too long. Thinking of language as more than a series of immaterial sonic apparitions or flat skeletons grafted onto paper or screens—the privilege of the hearing and the seeing—can make it more accessible to all. This is one way to keep using—instead of losing—our minds.

Plastic Words

Yuliya Komska

There is a language nightmare that haunts many fellow academics: that verbal concepts will get "reified," or pass into life, become real, material. From Latin *res*, thing. Like "res publica," a public thing or cause—a republic, that is.

One imagines these reified words waddling about clumsily. They bump into things and people, lean on walls in frustration at the end of the day. They are disheveled and bug-eyed, covered in embarrassing pajama-striped fuzz, grinning through their fangs, like the monsters in Maurice Sendak's *Where the Wild Things Are*. Would they be so dangerous? Perhaps. Unlike the words we now have, these could act, often upon us, with violence or kindness. But then, we also wouldn't be able to ignore them quite so easily. They would be public things, out in the open.

Police could lock them up, of course, but then word rights activists would sound the alarm immediately, and journalists would rush to cover the detention. The rest of us would call on politicians to intercede and insist on a fair jury trial and due process. If the curious beasts are later set free, we would celebrate the release for a few weeks, then forget about them sheepishly. If they do land behind bars, we would petition to have them transferred to a more adjectival detention facility where the reading lists are less heavily censored, so that *Freakonomics*, *The Memoirs of a Geisha*, and the pop-up edition of *A Charlie Brown Christmas* can keep the inmates company on dark winter nights. In brief, we would treat these material words like we treat other citizens of our republic. We would care, a tiny bit.

"Plastic words": the writer Samuel Beckett's turn of phrase, which I encountered briefly while writing about critique, stopped me in my tracks. That's what the reified words would be—plastic. Toying with the idea of the words' alternative lives in our midst (*The Secret Lives of Words*, as it were) was irresistible, but the experience wasn't all sweet. People, as the famous medieval historian Johan Huizinga wrote amid the tragic events of World War II, have a "play instinct" that extends over life's entirety, from sandbox to religious ritual to combat. The child, the athlete, the musician, the soldier during war games. All play "in complete earnest," some lighthearted, others serious (Huizinga 1949, p. 18). Languages, Huizinga noted, transport the ambivalence across cultures. Where doesn't play—*ludus*, in Latin—arise? Allusion, illusion, and, gasp, collusion—it is everywhere, often at the border between real and unreal, fair and foul (36). And so, entertaining the idea of plastic words was not an entirely frivolous pastime.

By "plastic" Beckett did not mean artificial but rather full-bodied. The epithet was intended not just for any words but for German words. Long and somber like a wooded path in a Romantic painting, heavy like *Weltschmerz*—world-weariness—and encumbered by veils, dress trains, and pins like a Wilhelmine dowager, they have the reputation of nearly bursting under the pressure of the multiple universes stacked within. Anglophone imaginations respond to them with bafflement. "There's got to be a German word for …," English-speakers would often say. An inveterate Germanist, I would naively offer one or fumble for it. It took me years to realize that people don't *actually* want to know what the word is. The question is only a turn of phrase, a joke.

I have tried to make peace with the discovery, but their disinterest still bothers me. Why not find out what that German word is? It is not so much about staging meetings with *German* words, I have come to realize while writing this book, as with *all* words, old and new, native and borrowed, short and long. Developing lasting, deep relationships with them. It's been difficult lately, even in the age of the online Super Dictionaries—Merriam-Webster, the OED, and others—and the various attendant Word of the Year rituals that make our Decembers more festive or, at times, dire. Where we used to consult the Chinese lunar calendar, we now wonder: will this be the year of the "'Face with Tears of Joy' emoji" or "antifa"? Most of these word look-ups are just word hook-ups, however, and the Super Dictionaries, for many of us, remain only verbal versions of Tinder. Non-committal.

If more words were plastic—rather, if more of us would perceive them as such—perhaps we would want to meet them more closely. Touch them. Try them on. Cuddle with them. Kick them in anger. Make sense of them and ourselves together, every day. The thought snuck up on me at a typewriter art show at the Pérez Art Museum in Miami, FL.

I have seen word art before. Concrete poetry, of course. One of the favorites is the Russian conceptualist Dmitri Prigov's "Man Cannot Live by Bread Alone…." The repeated sentence outlines an empty vodka bottle. John Baldessari, in *I Will Not Make Any More Boring Art* (1971), scribbled the line on a piece of paper 17 times. Yoko Ono issued simple commands, such as "Don't stop breathing!" Tracey Emin laced her considerably less zen neon inscriptions with sexual vulnerability. A digital print in the *Do Not Abandon Me* series (2009–2010), her piercing collaboration with Louise Bourgeois, shows a soigné nude in an orgasmic pose inside an oversized blood-red-hued pregnant woman's body. Underneath, the crooked inscription reads, "I WAИTED TO LOVE YOU MORE."

I admired these works as they emptied my mind or, in the last case, bludgeoned me. But they didn't touch me, and I didn't touch them. I didn't want to.

The typewriter art I wanted to touch. In several shades of ink, language shapeshifted, op-art-like. Letters, symbols, punctuation marks. In black against white, word clouds thickened and thinned. In blue, dashes formed intricate three-dimensional shapes that would have been at home in any constructivist's sketchbook. In burgundy, sign-drenched surfaces seemed to move together and apart again, like some Futurist time-space experiments.

Typewriters, according to the doyen of media theory Friedrich Kittler, mechanized the production of texts and necessitated immense industrial spaces where typewriters, the people, spent their days in incessant clatter. At the same time, they also let women into the very male world of text creation, recording, processing, and reproduction. They pried the door of the "Gutenberg galaxy"—the world of print—open for the previously excluded. And to both genders, they afforded "the possibility of rereading their writing through touch" (Kittler 1999, pp. 183–187).

Glued to our computers and smartphones, we constantly leach off this legacy as we type and swipe, oblivious to the possibilities that touch opens for the relationships between language and us. As I draw up a mental list of such missed opportunities, a playful essay by Theodor W. Adorno, "Punctuation Marks," comes to mind. In it, he, in effect, forecasts emoticons by imagining individual punctuation mark physiognomies, which he goes on to introduce in personal, almost familial terms (Adorno 1990). If dashes weren't limbless "furrows on the brow of [...] text," we could shake hands with them. We get to meet them in any case. Also, the film *The Arrival* occurs to me. There, alien language emanates in intensely embodied ink squirts, which humans immediately rush to decipher, first for securitarian reasons, but then, ostensibly, to communicate. By the end, there is a sense, though too obtrusively anthropomorphic, as we note earlier, that precisely touch has the power to compel and catalyze interactions with language.

So, what if we got over the fear of the reified, plastic words—and other symbols—and invited them to join our republic? We might care for them a tiny bit more.

Written in Blood
Michelle Moyd

Ceridwen Dovey's December 2017 *New Yorker* piece "The Mapping of Massacres" relates a harrowing history of Australia that has forced me to reckon in new ways with global histories of imperial violence and how they are memorialized. Dovey begins by describing the recent spate of toppling and defacing statues to "white men of empire," and in the United States, Confederate generals, who were "responsible for atrocities." Evoking Charlottesville and public demands for removal of a prominent statue of Robert E. Lee there, Dovey asks, "But when the statues come down, how might the atrocities themselves be publicly commemorated, rather than repressed?"

Dovey guides her readers on a sobering journey through the work of Australian historians, artists, and digital specialists who have made answering a version of this question their life's work. She starts with historian Lyndall Ryan, whose work on Tasmanian aboriginals had explored the consequences of imperial violence. As in many parts of the world where European imperial expansion took the form of violent conquest, aboriginal peoples who fought against the British in the Tasmanian War were massacred. In the 2000s, in what became known as the "History Wars," Australians grappled with how to tell the story of the conquest of Australia, and how to explain the position of aboriginal populations within that story. Inspired by social scientists like Jacques Sémelin, who after the 1995 Srebrenica massacre had turned to analyzing "massacre as a phenomenon," Ryan realized that the history she knew so well needed reframing within a much wider context of imperial violence. In reassessing her earlier work on the Tasmanian War, "Ryan concluded that there were not four massacres of Indigenous people but, in fact, more than forty." This shattering realization led her to undertake the daunting work of "map[ping] the site of every Australian colonial frontier massacre on an interactive Web site." By defining massacre as "the indiscriminate killing of six or more undefended people," and through meticulous research that found some 500 massacres of aboriginal peoples overall, Ryan opened up a new window into Australia's violent past. Her incomplete project, now available online, shows that layers of silence have shaped how generations of Australians have thought, selectively, about their history. And it does so in a visually overwhelming way, forcing people to reckon with the immense scale of violence perpetrated in the name of empire and state-making.

Beyond these stirring revelations, Dovey's essay also compels her readers to rethink authorship and history. Although professional historians like Lyndall Ryan play key roles in bringing such histories of violence to light, Dovey's piece shows the dimensions of human experience we miss by relying solely on archives, or the professional historian's authorial voice. Aboriginal artists and scholars like Aleshia Lonsdale, Judy Watson, Genevieve Grieves, and others are engaged in their own projects of recovering and memorializing aboriginal histories. In interviewing these women, Dovey draws out vital critical perspectives that challenge accepted histories, as well as the methodologies that create them. Lonsdale notes that aboriginal communities have their own memories of massacres that do not appear in the colonial record, and thus also do not appear on Ryan's map. Or at least, not yet.

One of the most exciting potentials of Ryan's project is restorative: she wants "to include massacres that aren't represented in written evidence but have been known about and passed down through memory and story by descendants of victims, survivors, and perpetrators." This is an admirable first step in the ongoing process of acknowledging that histories are always the result of contestation and reinterpretation that follow in the wake of disputes, whether major or minor. And Dovey's essay also urges reflection on what counts as history, making a convincing case for keeping the doors open to art, orality, and other forms as historical expressions. Judy Watson, for example, created an interactive art installation called "the names of places." It includes a map of massacres, incorporating indigenous memories of violence that might not appear in other representations. This kind of work serves as a necessary corrective to histories driven by colonial archives.

In my own archive-driven historical work, the issues raised in Dovey's piece emerge time and again. In using colonial records to study African soldiers who fought in imperial armies in the 1890s and later, I encounter many references to massacres perpetrated against African peoples, often addressed only in passing, as if the officers recording the violence thought nothing of it. And indeed, this is probably the truth of the matter. They either did not think anything of it, or they could not write about what they had done beyond a descriptive level. While general descriptors of "punitive raids," "pacification campaigns," and other euphemisms that indicate violent encounters appear with some frequency in historical accounts, it is rare to see these mentions developed into more textured, layered studies of the patterns that led to mass killings. And those who experienced the massacres and survived rarely get to tell their stories. Or perhaps it's more accurate to say that historians rarely hear these stories across the decades, through the smoothed out narratives of postcolonial independent nations. There are notable exceptions, of course, including works on massacres committed by the British in Kenya during Mau Mau, by a French military column in the Lake Chad region, and against citizens in postcolonial Angola (Anderson 2005; Elkins 2005; Taithe 2009; Pawson 2014).

But many more of these dark histories remain unexamined. Much work can be done to uncover what happened to communities that experienced massacres, to map them, and to incorporate indigenous narratives about them into our distant and secondary renditions of imperial conquest. Dovey's discussions with aboriginal artists and activists reveal that the violence of the past lives on in the memories of their descendants in untold ways. Historians work with evidence, and all too often, evidence means *written* evidence. But this is an impoverished way of understanding the past, and it leads to equally impoverished understandings of the present.

What hit me the hardest in Dovey's piece is this sentence: "Many existing place names around [Australia] are themselves a form of damning evidence, as the historian Ian Clark has noted in his own pioneering work on frontier massacres: Murderers Flat, Massacre Inlet, Murdering Gully,

Haunted Creek, Slaughterhouse Gully." In our ongoing often acrimonious discussions around who should be memorialized and how, we train our focus on objects that act as *containers* of memory—statues, plaques, steles, and various kinds of buildings, such as ossuaries. Or we focus on *markers* that show us where a specific past event happened. Germany's *Stolpersteine*—small brass plaques that are cobbled into pavements to mark the former home of a person or persons deported by the Nazi regime—are one of the most moving versions of this type of memorial. In thinking about correcting our approaches to who and what should be memorialized, we might draw inspiration from the insight provided by Ian Clark, referenced in the quote above. Just because memories of a violent past are unmarked does not mean they are unimportant or undeserving of recognition (Lichtenstein and Lichtenstein 2017, pp. 1–18; Nunn 2015). Instead, they are written in blood. Recognizing and mapping these sites with sensitivity to the narrative needs of the descendants of those killed or hurt by past violence is painful and painstaking work. But it is a potentially restorative kind of correction we can offer to those suffering in the present, and to those who will look back on the future and judge our efforts.

No
David Gramling

Bahia Shehab's ongoing, mobile artwork "A Thousand Times No" from 2015 has touched me like few other acts of linguistic disobedience have. Prompted by British curators to produce an artwork encapsulating Islamic Art in Europe over the past century, and to (please) do so using traditions of Arabic calligraphy, she decided to answer this invitation with the single Arabic word "No" ("لا"). But this "no" was not just "negative"—in the philosophical, critical, pessimistic, or even misanthropic tradition of negativity or negation. This لا was a creative, synthetic, traveling, historical, collective, collecting, and stunningly beautiful No. Shehab collected all of the instances she could find of the Arabic word لا over one and a half millennia—on pots, tapestries, parchment, buildings, clothing, prayer books, everywhere. Over the course of Shehab's artistic sojourn, Egypt erupted into revolution against its "pharaoh" president Hosni Mubarak, and the artist found that the collection she had worked to compile until that point was now prompting her, with all the weight and levity of the "no's" of the ages, to say "No to militarism," "No to a New Pharaoh," and "No to violence." By way of silk-screens and other materials, she transferred the images of the "No's" she had collected from Arab history onto contemporary Egyptian civic surfaces (walls, sidewalks, windows, barricades) and used these images to re-utter resistance and commitment in a moment of volatile and monumental political crisis.

During a period in which Egypt and other Arab countries contended with profound and violent political reconstitutions, which required of their citizens non-stop courage and fearlessness (despite exhaustion and disorientation), liberal White Americans and Europeans seemed to slide into a neoliberal idiom of compliance, opportunistic sloganeering, and free-market defeatism. In my own case, an if-you-can't-beat-em-talk-like-em strategy pervaded many of the decisions of my own early career, as downsizing was increasingly called "collaboration," precaritization of labor was called "being flexible," fiscalization was called "being responsible," and bilingualism and ethnic studies were dismissed in favor of a rebranded multilingualism and intercultural competence (Katznelson and Bernstein 2017). I did not say "no" to much of this. I did feel I had retained my critical sense of what was happening to the language within my profession and its institutions, but I was doing little to counter the effects of it on others—students, colleagues, public interlocutors.

A few weeks after the election of Donald Trump in the United States, I was scheduled to give a lecture in London on my book, *The Invention of Monolingualism*. Though monolingualism, the topic of the day, seemed indeed to be somehow at the tragic core of America's addiction to placing the interests of plutocrats over the needs of its people, it was more important to me on that early December 2016 day in London to be honest, before an international audience, about how generally undone I and my friends were about Trump, about the emboldened and unburdened idioms of disdain joyriding at the wheel of our country's government, and about another impending decade of deferred hopes for justice and a habitable planet for all.

In that month before Trump's inauguration, and in full view of the ensuing national trainwreck, I shared the following thoughts at the Transnationalizing Modern Languages conference, organized by the Italianists Loredana Polezzi and Charles Burdett:

I didn't write my book *The Invention of Monolingualism* in a post-Brexit, post-Trump age, but I suppose I did write it amid all of the interlocking conditions that led us here. So far, I've found that only very little of what I had written and suspected about the structure, substance, and historical contingencies of monolingualism and multilingualism has been overturned by these momentous events. For my part, the gutting, vexing disabusal of false comfort that I, my students, and colleagues have gone through in the United States in the last month has encouraged me (after some moments of profound doubt, dread, and directionlessness) to quicken my step, to polish up my heart, and to become more synthetic and regenerative in my own commitments and collaborations in the modern languages as a scholar, teacher, friend, brother, sister, and also often as a stranger or resister.

Today, just as a year ago, whether we opt to call monolingualism a myth, a pathology, a paradigm, a relic, or a sham, I believe more than ever that it is (despite our wishes) woven into the most minute and sophisticated political structures of contemporary life, and it is clearly not as yet inclined to be waved off the stage by a "multilingual turn" in one or another discipline—whether applied linguistics or comparative literature. Monolingualism has a lot of power and cleverness behind it. It even has, as I hope to show, its very own versions of cosmopolitanism, globalism, multilingualism, and transnationalism. Monolingualism does not want us to, as Loredana Polezzi has so elegantly put it, change the DNA of modern languages. Monolingualism does, I believe, want to flatten the DNA of modern languages, make modern languages tokenistic and serviceable and user-friendly, but it does not want to change the DNA of modern languages, in the rich methodological, embodied, and lyrical ways that I take Loredana Polezzi to mean that phrase. I think it is also for this reason important to distinguish monolingualism at the outset from other powerful notions about language— including linguistic purism, imperialism, standardization, nationalism, and the like.

One thing I feel I have not done adequately in my book however is to make any concrete suggestions about how and why to dismantle, disinvent, or disenchant monolingualism. This was in two senses a quite deliberate abstention, though also perhaps an indulgent one: the first reason I did not talk much in the book about disinventing monolingualism was that I am not a policy maker, political operative, or a program builder. At least at this point in my career, I am a critic and a teacher, and therefore am neither by disposition nor by training particularly equipped for the strategic, technical work of disinvention. And further, I've long felt that modern languages and applied linguistics scholarship over the last two decades has already been more than sanguine in its bid to disestablish monolingual paradigms, and I wanted instead to do some rather agnostic and unprogrammatic work with the concept of monolingualism, work that was neither positivistic nor diagnostic nor fault-finding. So I seem to have refrained quite assiduously from talking in the book about actively disinventing monolingualism, in the present progressive tense, But maybe now, with you today, it's time to change my tack a bit and, as Allen Ginsberg wrote in a similarly ominous moment, 'put my queer shoulder to the wheel,' too (2016).

Since that day in London, I have become more cautious and skeptical about my own personal, civic, and professional role in ratifying what Rachel Greenwald Smith has called "compromise aesthetics" (2014). Unaccustomed as I am nonetheless to saying "no"—as a crucial potentiating condition for putting my own queer shoulder to the wheel—I take great comfort, guidance, and provocation in the work of Bahia Shehab, who has for me turned negation into an eloquent, beautiful, and social act. Neither a cause for shame nor an indication of laziness or copping out, saying "no" is often the first step toward a better answer—one that may never emerge, but is worth waiting and fighting for. Together with the "excessive yes" (Mackin 2016, p. 165) so beautifully exemplified in the work of Palestinian artists like Emily Jacir and of the Black Lives Matter movements, the honest and unequivocal "no" is a crucial interjection for any courageous idiom of linguistic disobedience.

References

Adorno, Theodor W. "Punctuation Marks." Translated by Sherry Weber. *The Antioch Review* 48, no. 3 (Summer 1990): 300–305.

Anderson, David. *Histories of the Hanged: The Dirty War in Kenya and the End of Empire*. New York: W.W. Norton, 2005.

Crary, Jonathan. *Suspensions of Perception: Attention, Spectacle, and Modern Culture*. Cambridge, MA: The MIT Press, 1999.

Dovey, Ceridwen. "The Mapping of Massacres." *The New Yorker*. December 6, 2017.

Elkins, Caroline. *Imperial Reckoning: The Untold Story of Britain's Gulag in Kenya*. New York: Holt, 2005.

Gramling, David. "Disinventing Monolingualism in the Modern Languages." Keynote Lecture at the Transnationalizing Modern Languages Conference. Italian Cultural Institute London. December 4, 2016.

Greenwald Smith, Rachel. "Six Propositions on Compromise Aesthetics." *The Account*. Fall 2014.

Hardt, Michael and Antonio Negri. *War and Democracy in the Age of Empire*. London: Penguin Books, 2004.

Huizinga, Johan. *Homo Ludens: A Study of the Play-Element in Culture*. Translated by R. F. C. Hull. London: Routledge & Kegan Paul, 1949.

Jamison, Leslie. "Does Recovery Kill Great Writing?" *The New York Times Magazine*, March 13, 2018. https://www.nytimes.com/2018/03/13/magazine/does-recovery-kill-great-writing.html.

Katznelson, Noah and Katie Bernstein. "Rebranding Bilingualism: The Shifting Discourses of Language Education Policy in California's 2016 election." *Linguistics and Education* 40 (2017): 11–26.

Kittler, Friedrich. *Gramophone, Film, Typewriter*. Translated by Geoffrey Winthrop-Young and Michael Wutz. Stanford, CA: Stanford University Press, 1999.

Lichtenstein, Andrew and Alex Lichtenstein. *Marked Unmarked Remembered: A Geography of American Memory*. West Virginia University Press, 2017.

Mackin, Glenn. "Black Lives Matter and the Concept of the Counterworld." *Philosophy and Rhetoric* 49, no. 4 (2016): 459–481.

Nunn, Cedric. *Unsettled: The 100 Year War of Resistance by Xhosa against Boer and British*. Brooklyn: Archipelago Books, 2015.

Pawson, Lara. *In the Name of the People: Angola's Forgotten Massacre*. London: I. B. Tauris, 2014.

Ripley, Amanda. *The Unthinkable: Who Survives When the Disaster Strikes*. New York: Crown Publishers, 2008.

Shapiro, Ari. "Author Leslie Jamison Hopes to Change How People Think About Creativity and Recovery." *NPR*, March 30, 2018. https://www.npr.org/2018/03/30/598386440/author-leslie-jamison-hopes-to-change-how-people-think-about-creativity-and-reco.

Shehab, Bahia. *A Thousand Times No: A Visual History of the Lam-Elif.* Amsterdam: Khatt Books, 2015.

Taithe, Bertrand. *The Killer Trail: A Colonial Scandal in the Heart of Africa.* Oxford: Oxford University Press, 2009.

Teicher, Martin H., Jacqueline A. Samson, Yi-Shin Sheu, Ann Polcari, and Cynthia E. McGreenery. "Hurtful Words: Association of Exposure to Peer Verbal Abuse with Elevated Psychiatric Symptom Scores and Corpus Callosum Abnormalities." *American Journal of Psychiatry* 167 (2010): 1464–1471.

Index[1]

[1] Note: Page numbers followed by 'n' refer to notes.

© The Author(s) 2019
Y. Komska et al., *Linguistic Disobedience*,
https://doi.org/10.1007/978-3-319-92010-8

CPSIA information can be obtained
at www.ICGtesting.com
Printed in the USA
LVOW13s0325200718

584351LV00019B/361/P

9 783319 920092